"Doc"

Memories of Edward C. Farmer

By

Martena Gunnlaugsson Koken

Front cover picture;
Milwaukee Journal, dated 1 June 1975, R. Brodzeller photographer, © 2007 Journal
Sentinel Inc., reproduced with permission

ISBN 1-4392-1016-0

LCCN: 2008908148

Graphics and Cover Design by Koken Farm

Visit our Website at: www.kokenfarm.com

*"There was nothing specialized about my practice. I was expected to come when called, know what I was doing when I got there, and fix whatever went wrong." ***

--*Doc Farmer*

* Quote from a 1974 *Door County Advocate* article by Keta Steebs

"Doc"

Foreword
(From Doc's daughter Jane)

My family lived on Washington Island, Wisconsin, where I spent my early years in the 1950s. Dad was the doctor. Washington Island is a very special place to live. Everyone knows everyone, and you are probably related to dozens of folks.

Even when we moved to Sister Bay, on the mainland, Dad remained as the only doctor north of Sturgeon Bay. The extended family of friends and neighbors was spread a few more miles out.

In 1975, the Milwaukee Journal featured an article in a Sunday issue, entitled: A Man Called "Doc". After reading that article, I thought that there were many more stories that could be told.

After receiving a story about my father, that Martena had written and read on Public Radio, I was so pleased. Martena mentioned that she would like to collect stories from Dad's former patients, colleagues and friends for a book. My reaction was "Yes! That would be wonderful!"

Martena has done a great job researching, requesting, collecting stories and writing this book of memories about my father, Doc Farmer.

Jane Farmer Kane

Acknowledgments

Special thanks to Jane Farmer Kane for all her collaboration and loving input; to Pete Oleson for his beyond-the-call legwork; to my husband Rip, for his photographic skills; to Joyce Pettis for her untiring editing; to Barbara Ellefson WI Archives; to Dan Grooms, archivist at Midwestern; to Kari Fitzgerald Brandt, Norbert Blei, Keta Steebs, Hannes Andersen, Adeline Edmund's daughter, Lynn Mattke, and Florence Jess' son, Butch, for permission to reprint their Doc stories; to the many friends and patients of Doc who took the time to tell their stories and especially to Doc Farmer.

Thanks Doc; we are eternally grateful for your loving care.

Jane Farmer Kane and Martena Gunnlaugsson Koken

Contents

Memories of Edward C. Farmer

Preface

I became interested in writing Doc Farmer's story when I wrote and recorded a four minute presentation for the Sundial Writer's Corner on the public radio station, WLRH, in Huntsville, Alabama. I sent the story to Doc's daughters, Jane and Sara. Jane was very enthusiastic about the prospect of a book about her father. Sara was not interested.

I talked to my mom, Nora Gunnlaugsson, about her memories, and she suggested that I talk to relatives and friends to see what they remembered about Doc. Soon I had many accounts of Doc's spirit of service. His dedication to healing surpassed anything I could have invented. Heroes are not the guys and gals with the cape or mask. Heroes are the people who plunge into life and strive with all their might to make it better. Doc was such a hero. He not only plunged in; he swam his whole existence in the murky water of medicine, politics, and life and death.

Doc Farmer was one of those "true grit salt of the earth" compassionate healers. His story deserves to be recorded, for it is a prescription for good medicine--a remedy for the common cold practitioner. Doc was a real Norman Rockwell character, a true healer and medicine man. If Jesus built a bridge with two boards and three nails, then Doc crossed that bridge many times on a wing and a prayer.

Who am I to think I can write Doc's story? I am from Washington Island in Wisconsin, where Doc spent the better part of twenty years. My father, Maynard Gunnlaugsson, was an Islander who hunted with Doc. My mother, Nora, chose Doc to deliver her five girls. I was the third of the deliveries and being born in January, I was blessed to be welcomed into the cold Wisconsin winter by Doc's warm loving hands.

May my hand be as kind to Doc in delivery of his life as he was in delivering mine, and may my words be as well chosen and well written as Doc's chosen field and dedicated life.

Dr. Edward Clayton Farmer

Doc Farmer Doc farmer Doc Farmer Doc farmer Doc Farmer Doc farmer Doc Farmer Doc farmer Doc Farmer Doc farmer Doc Farmer Doc farmer

2

Sepia-Colored Dust

As Aired on Sundial Writer's Corner in 2006

I love strolling in antique shops. Each item stirs up the sepia-colored dust of memories. One such stirring occurred when I happened upon a very old, very weary worn black leather doctor's satchel. The yesterdays came floating into my mind's eye like motes glistening in the sun.

When the dust settled, it took the shape of a bushy mustachioed country doctor from my childhood, Dr. Farmer. His specialty was house calls. Sadly, like the black leather bag, doctors like Doc Farmer have all but disappeared.

Oh, for you to see this wise old bespectacled healer, a Norman Rockwell character if there ever was one--scruffy little mustache, bushy brows, spectacles resting on a generous nose, warm hands and a doubly warm heart.

His heh, heh, heh, laugh of glee was contained in his throat—like a ventriloquist's voice—probably because there was always a pipe clamped in his teeth. I still envision him tamp, tamp, tamping that pipe in a pestle and mortar sort of way when pondering a particularly difficult situation. And those situations varied widely, from delivering babies, to delivering osteopathic adjustments, to delivering freedom from pain of rotten teeth and infected tonsils, to delivering advice, hope and sometimes miracles.

My sister, Kathy, was one of those miracles. Doc Farmer had already delivered four girls to my mom and dad. On the fourth girl, my sister, Maynette, Doc had bet mom two bits this one was for sure a boy. Although she never received that quarter, she was repaid a thousand-fold with this fifth delivery.

Kathy was premature. Her lungs were underdeveloped. When Doc consulted the Green Bay doctors, they told him there was nothing to be done. Preparing for the inevitable, mom had Kathy baptized. But with Doc and his wife, Ruby, as godparents, magic couldn't be too far away. Doc dug deep down into his little black bag of tricks and came up with a suggestion: 'would mom and dad consider letting him try a "liver" shot?' Whatever that shot was--he gave part to Kathy and the rest to mom--it did the trick! Kathy turned the corner. She just turned her fifty-third corner of life in May.

My sister Jeanie remembers having a really bad toothache one evening. Even though Doc was having a dinner party, when mom called, he said, "Sure, bring her on over." Jeanie says she remembers trying to decide if she should wear a dress or pants, pants or dress.

Doc Farmer Doc farmer Doc Farmer Doc farmer Doc Farmer Doc farmer Doc Farmer Doc farmer Doc Farmer Doc farmer Doc Farmer Doc farmer Doc Farmer Doc farmer

4

When Doc yanked that tooth, Jeanie almost fainted. Doc grabbed her by the ankles and held her upside down in front of all those dinner guests. Forget the tooth, forget the pain, all Jeanie could think was, "Whew, am I glad I wore pants!!"

When I was about 5 years old, Doc removed my tonsils. I remember being wrapped in sheets like a mummy, the terrible smell of the ether, and counting. The next thing I knew, I was lying in my parent's bed and mom was asking if I'd like some ice cream. Doc put those old tonsils in formaldehyde in a jar and I kept those things in the medicine cabinet for years. Can you imagine opening the cabinet for the toothpaste and having nasty "something drug in from the swamp" tonsils staring back at you?

Oh, and before I pull over on this trip down memory lane, I have to tell you. Doc moved off the Island around 1957. In 1960, my mom was pregnant for a sixth time. A different doctor delivered my brother. She wrote a little note to Doc Farmer and it went like this:

Dear Doc,

I knew all along it was your fault, we now have a boy! By the way, you still owe me a quarter.

Love, Nora

Doc Farmer Doc farmer Doc Farmer Doc farmer Doc Farmer Doc farmer Doc Farmer Doc farmer Doc Farmer Doc farmer Doc Farmer Doc farmer

5

I bet he had a heh, heh, heh, laugh over that one.

Doc Farmer's common sense approach to doctoring, his willingness to try anything, his knowledge, faith and little black bag filled with compassion stirred up a lot of dust along the country roads of Washington Island and all of Door County. I bet if you look hard enough at the star filled night sky there is a Farmer constellation stirring up some interstellar dust still today.

Doc Farmer Doc farmer Doc Farmer Doc farmer Doc Farmer Doc farmer Doc Farmer Doc farmer Doc Farmer Doc farmer Doc Farmer Doc farmer

6

"It is quite a three pipe problem, and I beg that you won't speak to me for fifty minutes."

-Sherlock Holmes in 'The Red-headed League'

Pestle and Mortar

In the world of Dr. Edward C. Farmer, his pipe was the pestle and mortar of any prescriptive diagnosis. Like Sherlock Holmes, Doc ruminated over mysteries by smoking, chewing on or tamping his pipe. Like Sherlock's pipe, Doc's pipe was his counselor. For us patients, it was a symbol of powerful medicine.

Like a talisman, Doc carried that pipe wherever he roamed. A whiff of that tobacco smell, as he entered the room, was ether to pain and suffering because you knew Doc could fix whatever ailed you. The smoke was like the steam rising from Doc's brain as he used his powers of deduction. And, in Doc's hand, if the stem of that pipe was pointing directly at you, that pipe became an exclamation point! No telling how many pipes Doc left, along with his prescription of health, because he was constantly setting his pipe down and forgetting it.

The pipe wasn't the only similarity between Sherlock Holmes and Doc. They were both mystery detectives—Sherlock solving the mystery of crime and Doc solving the mystery of

Doc Farmer Doc farmer Doc Farmer Doc farmer Doc Farmer Doc farmer Doc Farmer Doc farmer Doc Farmer Doc farmer Doc Farmer Doc farmer

7

illness; they were both blessed with wisdom—
'an infinite capacity for taking pains'; they had
definite opinions about the right and wrong
ways of doing things with no tolerance for
bureaucracy; they both took their calling
seriously and dedicated their lives to peoples'
ills; they both shared an English ancestry and
both of their characters were shaped by
medicine.

Although Sherlock Holmes was a fictional
character, author Sir Arthur Conan Doyle was a
physician and based Sherlock's character on one
of his teachers, a real doctor, Dr. Joseph Bell.
Bell is described by Martin Booth in his book,
The Doctor and the Detective, as

*"A sparse and lean man with the long and
sensitive fingers of a musician, sharp grey eyes
twinkling with shrewdness, an angular nose with a
chin to match, unkempt dark hair and a high pitched
voice. Blessed with a wry sense of humour, he spoke
precisely and clearly...More than a medical man, he
was also a widely read amateur poet, a competent
raconteur (teller of anecdotes), a keen sportsman, a
naturalist and a bird-watcher....He was a very skilful
surgeon, but his strong point was diagnosis, not only
of disease, but of occupation and character.*

*...It was Bell's dictum that a doctor had to be not
only learned but immensely interpretive of all relevant*

Doc Farmer Doc farmer Doc Farmer Doc farmer Doc Farmer Doc farmer Doc Farmer Doc farmer Doc Farmer Doc farmer Doc Farmer Doc farmer

8

features of a patient. Diagnosis, he taught, was not just made by visual observation but also by the employment of all the senses: do not just look at a patient, he advised, but feel him, probe him, listen to him, smell him. Only then could a diagnosis be attempted."

Doc Farmer and Dr. Bell (alias Sherlock Holmes) seemed to be 'twin brothers of different mothers'; both great diagnosticians, great believers in the whole person approach to healing, and both sticklers for the facts. An interesting fact is that Dr. Bell was the honorary surgeon to King Edward VII, for whom Doc Edward Farmer was named.

Since Sherlock Holmes' story begins "Being a reprint from the reminiscences of John H. Watson, M.D." we will also begin Edward Clayton Farmer's story this way:

Being a recall from the reminiscences of family, friends and patients of Edward Clayton Farmer D.O., we are attempting to tell the true story of Doc to the best of our memories, the best of our ability, and with the best of intentions.

Edward C. Farmer, Doc to most, was born in Sault Ste Marie, Ontario, Canada, on December 23, 1904. His parents were George Henry and Sarah Nott Farmer. His maternal grandparents were from the Nottingham area in

Doc Farmer Doc farmer Doc Farmer Doc farmer Doc Farmer Doc farmer Doc Farmer Doc farmer Doc Farmer Doc farmer Doc Farmer Doc farmer

9

England. His paternal grandmother, Magdalena was born in Alsace-Lorraine and Grandfather Henry was born in Basingstoke, England. Henry served in the Crimean war; he was wounded by shrapnel from a Russian shelling and was most proud of being nursed back to health by Florence Nightingale.

Jane Farmer Kane, Doc's daughter, wrote a college essay about her great-grandfather Henry and his Crimean War experience.

"The pride in my father's voice is what I remember:

'My grandfather, your great-grandfather, was decorated by Her Majesty Queen Victoria,' he would begin. Father painted a very romantic picture of his grandfather fighting for England in the Crimean War.

Henry Farmer, my great-grandfather, was a farmer's son, from the village of Basingstoke, just west of London, in England. He signed on with the 7th Regiment of Royal Fusiliers at the age of eighteen, April 1, 1866. Henry stood five feet four inches tall. The flintlock musket with bayonet that he carried was longer than he was tall. In my mind's eye, I picture this brown-haired young recruit looking for adventure, full of enthusiasm to go wherever his queen would send him.

...On October 25, 1855, the young infantryman, Henry Farmer, fell victim to a Russian

Doc Farmer Doc farmer Doc Farmer Doc farmer Doc Farmer Doc farmer Doc Farmer Doc farmer Doc Farmer Doc farmer Doc Farmer Doc farmer

10

shelling. Shrapnel from an exploding cannonball peppered his face. The wounded and unconscious soldier was taken by an ox-drawn wagon ambulance to the quay in Balaclava. From the dock the wounded were placed shoulder to shoulder on the open wooden deck of a ship. On their journey across the Black Sea to the hospital there were no drugs or dressings and only one blanket to protect and comfort them.

At the hospital the downed fighter found he was in the most capable care of the famous nurse, Florence Nightingale. My great-grandfather told no stories of battles or the sufferings of war. He only spoke of Miss Nightingale and how the men 'worshipped'' her.

Recovered, but permanently disabled from the loss of his right eye, Henry returned to England. An honorable discharge and good conduct badge were issued after one year and 339 days of service. The Regimental Board recommended the Crimea Medal, inscribed with 'Sebastopol' be awarded to the young veteran.

...This family treasure continues to be proudly displayed with one of Henry's grandsons, Clayton Farmer..."

Although the Farmers migrated to Canada, they were proud of their English heritage. At the time Doc was born in 1904, Edward VII was King of England, so Doc, as the seventh son of George and Sarah, was named

Edward. Growing up on a farm, he learned the ethic of hard work, how to economize, and how to grow food without poisonous chemicals

Eventually, there were eleven siblings, George, Robert, Wesley, William (called Wilburn), Horace, Rose, Chester, Edward, Florence, Martha and Sarah.

Photo taken of Farmer Family in Canada circa 1914. George and Sarah bound the family on each end.

Edward C. Farmer

Doc Farmer Doc farmer Doc Farmer Doc farmer Doc Farmer Doc farmer Doc Farmer Doc farmer Doc Farmer Doc farmer Doc Farmer Doc farmer

12

"You're like a surgeon who wants every symptom before he can give his diagnosis."

--Sherlock Holmes in 'The Problem of Thor Bridge'

Becoming Doc

Doc's schooling consisted of twenty-four hours of high school credits, two years Collegiate Institute, and one year of Special Technical Courses in Science and Math (algebra, geometry, trigonometry and practical shop work) at the Saulte Ste Marie Technical School and five years study at the Chicago College of Osteopathy (now Midwestern University in Downers Grove, Illinois)

Chicago College of Osteopathy

Doc Farmer Doc farmer Doc Farmer Doc farmer Doc Farmer Doc farmer Doc Farmer Doc farmer Doc Farmer Doc farmer Doc Farmer Doc farmer

13

Part of the story of how Edward became Doc is told by Norbert Blei in his book, *Door Way:*

"As a young man, Doc was a machinist and went to school to become a mechanical engineer. But he recalls the time how his father got hurt on the farm, threw his neck out of place, and was straightened out by a visiting osteopath from Chicago. For some reason, young Edward Farmer was rather impressed with the kind of body mechanics an osteopath could perform. The osteopath, in turn, encouraged him. 'Why don't you come down to Chicago and go to school?' he advised.

This is exactly what Ed Farmer did in 1923, enrolling in The Chicago College of Osteopathy for a period of five years. "

Top Row: Parker, Johnson, Hoover, Pryor, Farmer, Hostetler, W. R. Hinsperger, Squier, C. V. Hinsperger, Thomas
Second Row: Corey, Dygert, Moore, Copley, Frantz, Crus
Bottom Row: Girvan, M. Walstrom, Wersemer, Moses, Cowan, Ray, Musselman, Perkins, Jedlicher, E. Walstrom

Prefreshman class at Chicago College of Osteopathy
(Doc last row center)

Doc Farmer Doc farmer Doc Farmer Doc farmer Doc Farmer Doc farmer Doc Farmer Doc farmer Doc Farmer Doc farmer Doc Farmer Doc farmer

14

Doc's dad sent him on a train to Chicago with $500. Doc learned how to survive on his own hundreds of miles from his home in Canada.

Doc's Fraternity (Doc upper left corner)

His Chicago College of Osteopathy records attest to his diligence and desire to excel.

Doc Farmer Doc farmer Doc Farmer Doc farmer Doc Farmer Doc farmer Doc Farmer Doc farmer Doc Farmer Doc farmer Doc Farmer Doc farmer

15

THE JUNIOR YEAR

Course	Year	Grade	Attendance	Instructor
The First Quarter				
Diagnosis 4 (Intermediate Physical Diagnosis)	1926	75	96	Downing
Surgery 1 (The Principles of Surgery, first part)	"	89	96	Collins
Orthopedic Surgery 1	"	81	100	Zaph
Gynecology 1 (Elementary Gynecology, first half)	"	85	90	Dunning
Obstetrics 1 (The Physiology of Pregnancy)	"	80	95	Dunning
Pediatrics 1 (Elementary Pediatrics)	"	90	96	Wells
Dietetics 1 (Diet in Health)	"	92	90	MacGregor
Technique 2	"	88	100	Schwab
Practice 4 (Diseases of the Stomach)	"	94	100	MacGregor
Practice 7 (Diseases of the Urinary System)	"	84	100	Sands
Practice 8 (Diseases of the Respiratory Tract)	1928	85	100	Clarke
Practice 9 (Osteopathic Gymnastics, first half)	1926	80	100	Gour
Practice 11 (Applied Osteopathy, first part)	quired			
Technique 2 (Osteopathic Applied Pathology)	1926	88	80	MacBain
Technique 8 (Principles of Osteopathic Technique, first half)	1926	92	100	Fryette
Treating 1 (Sixty Clinical Treatments)	1926	85	90	Peckham
Pathology 4 (Six Autopsies)	equired			
The Second Quarter				
Diagnosis 5 (Advanced Physical Diagnosis)	1927	85	97	Downing
Surgery 2 (The Principles of Surgery, second part)	"	82	100	Collins
Surgery 4 (General and Local Anesthesia)	1927	86	80	Peckham
X-Rays 1	1927	75	100	Hoskins
Gynecology 2 (Elementary Gynecology, second half)	"	80	100	Dunning
Obstetrics 2 (The Physiology of Labor and the Puerperium	"	78	100	Dunning
Pediatrics 2 (Intermediate Pediatrics)	"	95	100	Wells
Dietetics 2 (Diet in Disease)	"	97	100	MacGregor
Technique 6	"	96	94	Shain
Practice 5 (Diseases of the Liver and Pancreas)	"	94	100	MacGregor
Practice 10 (Osteopathic Gymnastics, second half)	"	90	100	Gour
Practice 12 (Applied Osteopathy, second part)	required			
Ortho. Surgery 2	1927	75	100	Zaph
Practice 15 (Diseases of the Bones and Joints)	1928	95	100	Wells
Technique 3 (Osteopathic Diagnosis)	1926	90	96	MacBain
Treating 2 (Sixty Clinical Treatments)	1927	85	90	Peckham
Technique 3	1927	78	100	Schwab
The Third Quarter				
Diagnosis 6 (Differential Diagnosis)	1927	87	97	Downing
Surgery 3 (The Principles of Surgery, third part)	"	82	93	Collins
Surgery Technique 7b	"	94	100	Shain
Surgery 8 (Orthopedics)	"	85	100	Gour
Surgery 9 (Orthopedic Surgery)	"	80	100	Zaph
Gynecology 3 (Intermediate Gynecology)	"	84	100	Dunning
Obstetrics 3 (The Hygiene and Conduct of Pregnancy and Labor)	"	96	95	Hanavan
Pediatrics 3 (Advanced Pediatrics)	"	95	95	Wells
Dietetics 3 (Combinations of Diet)	"	96	100	MacGregor
Practice 6 (Diseases of the Intestines)	"	94	100	MacGregor
Practice 13 (Applied Osteopathy, third part)	required			
Practice 16 (Diseases of the Ductless Glands and Metabolism)	1927	88	96	Wells
Practice 17 (Diseases of the Blood and Vascular System)	1926	85	92	Merrithew
Technique 4 (Soft Tissue Adjustment)	1927	86	90	Schwab
Technique 9 (Principles of Osteopathic Technique, second half) 7a	"	85	100	Fryette
Treating 3 (Sixty Clinical Treatments)	1927	80	80	Peckham
Pathology Dermatology	1927	80	84	Wells

No student is a Senior until he has completed all the work listed above.

Doc Farmer Doc farmer Doc Farmer Doc farmer Doc Farmer Doc farmer Doc Farmer Doc farmer Doc Farmer Doc farmer Doc Farmer Doc farmer Doc Farmer Doc farmer

16

THE SENIOR YEAR

Course	p Year	Grade	Attendance	Instructor
The First Quarter Ophthalmology	1927	90	88	Wells
Diagnosis 7 (Clinical Diagnosis, first part)	1927	83	84	MacBain
Surgery 10 (General Surgery: the Bones and Joints)	"	83	98	Zaph
Surgery 11 (General Surgery: the Genito-Urinary Organs)	"	83	98	Zaph
Surgery 16 (Clinic)	"	83	98	Zaph
Gynecology 4 (Clinic)	"	90	83	Collins
Obstetrics 4 (The Pathology of Pregnancy) 4a	"	83	91	Hanavan
Obstetrics 7 (Clinic; two Confinement Cases) 4b	"	84	100	Elfrink
Pediatrics 4 (Children's Clinic)	"	95	95	Proctor
Practice 18 (Psychotherapy, first part)	"	75	92	Schoolman
Practice 21 (Diseases of the Nervous System, first part)	"	84	100	Inwood
Practice 24 (Venereal Diseases)	926	100	100	Greer
Diseases of the Head and Neck 1 Physiotherapy	1927	95	100	Boehm
Jurisprudence 1	926	79	80	Pleck
Technique 5 (Osseous Adjustment) 8	1927	90	90	Fryette
Technique 10 14	"	75	96	McDonough
Technique 11	"	75	100	Morris
Treating 4 (Sixty Clinical Treatments)	1927	85	85	Peckham
Diagnosis Acute and Infectious Diseases	1927	94	95	Proctor

Comparative Therapeutics	1928	90	96	Hoskins
The Second Quarter Technique 12	"	75	80	Morris
Diagnosis 8 (Clinical Diagnosis, second part)	"	77	84	Robuck
Surgery 12 (General Surgery: the Digestive Tract)	"	88	100	Zaph
Surgery 13 (General Surgery: the Abdomen)	"	88	100	Zaph
Surgery 17 (Clinic)	"	89	90	Collins
Gynecology 5 (Clinic)	"	88	90	Elfrink
Obstetrics 5 (The Pathology of Labor)	"	88	92	Hanavan
Obstetrics 8 (Clinic; two Confinement Cases)	"	95	95	Proctor
Pediatrics 5 (Children's Clinic)	"	75	100	Schoolman
Practice 19 (Psychotherapy, second part)	"	90	100	Inwood
Practice 22 (Diseases of the Nervous System, second part)	1927	85	94	Hoskins
Practice 25 (Comparative Therapeutics)	1928	95	100	Deason
Diseases of the Head and Neck 2	927	79	90	Pleck
Jurisprudence 2	1928	90	98	Peckham
Technique 6 (Advanced Osteopathic Technique) Appendicular	"	90	100	Peckham
Technique 12	"	85	85	Peckham
Treating 5 (Sixty Clinical Treatments) Diagnosis 66	1928	79	98	MacBain
Acute and Infectious Dis.	1928	91	100	Proctor
Technique 15	1928	85	96	MacBain
The Third Quarter Diagnosis 7a	1928	88	94	Robuck
Diagnosis 9 (Clinical Diagnosis, third part)	"	84	100	MacBain
Surgery 14 (General Surgery: the Skin, N. ..., and Glands)	"	90	100	Zaph
Surgery 15 (General Surgery: the Head, Neck, and Thorax)				
Surgery 18 (Clinic) Antiseptics, Narcotics	927	80	100	Zaph
Gynecology 6 (Clinic)	928	88	90	Collins
Obstetrics 6 (The Pathology of the Puerperium)	"	95	88	Hanavan
Obstetrics 9 (Clinic; two Confinement Cases)	"	85	90	Elfrink
Pediatrics 6 (Children's Clinic)	"	90	100	Proctor
Practice 20 (Psychotherapy, third part)	"	85	90	Schoolman
Practice 23 (Diseases of the Nervous System, third part)	"	97	100	Inwood
Practice 26 (Acute and Infectious Diseases)	1928	87	90	Proctor
Diseases of the Head and Neck 3	"	80	100	Deason
Jurisprudence 3	927	75	90	Pleck
Technique 7 (Advanced Osteopathic Technique)	1928	85	100	Fryette
Technique 13	"	80	100	Morris
Technique 14	"	95	95	Peckham
Treating 6 (Sixty Clinical Treatments) Anatomy Review	"	85	85	Peckham
Bedside Technique	"	95	95	Peckham
	"	75	100	Gaddis

Even back in college days, Doc seemed to have trouble with 'jurisprudence'—the theory and philosophy of law. Anyone who knew Doc could see him standing up to Professor Pleck disputing the right and wrong of legal situations, confronting bureaucratic rule and protecting the rights of the 'little' guy. Doc, being one of the 'little' guys, knew the disadvantages of the poor and middle classes. He could have stayed in the Chicago area but chose his practice in rural communities.

Standing up for rights became Doc's mission in life, especially since Doctors of Osteopathy did not have the same privileges as M.D.'s. According to the Illinois Osteopathic Medical Society website, "the first legislative recognition of Osteopathy in Illinois is dated April 21, 1899. D.O.s were examined by the Medical Board as 'Other Practitioners' and could not be called doctors and had no legal rights. By 1923 (the year Doc started college), the law was changed so the Doctors of Osteopathic Medicine would be examined in Obstetrics and could legally practice Obstetrics.

...For more than half a century (from 1903-1955) Osteopathic physicians in Illinois were forced to practice under the handicap of a limited license. Then in the spring of 1955, the Illinois Supreme Court handed down a decision approving the Chicago College of Osteopathy as a school qualified to teach medicine and surgery

Doc Farmer Doc farmer Doc Farmer Doc farmer Doc Farmer Doc farmer Doc Farmer Doc farmer Doc Farmer Doc farmer Doc Farmer Doc farmer

18

in all of its branches." According to Ida Sorci, in the Library/Archives department of the American Osteopathic Association, Wisconsin passed unlimited practice laws in 1949.

Doc's Qualifying Certificate

For Doc, practicing from 1929 to 1949 under a 'limited license' and 'with limited legal rights', jurisprudence became a highly contested topic and produced a rebel country doctor. His formal education taught him a 'whole person' approach to medicine combined with the ideal of 'unity of all body parts', and a philosophy of preventive medicine. This preventive medicine meant not focusing on disease but on eating right, exercising, and maintaining nerve, muscle

Doc Farmer Doc farmer Doc Farmer Doc farmer Doc Farmer Doc farmer Doc Farmer Doc farmer Doc Farmer Doc farmer Doc Farmer Doc farmer

19

and bone balance through manipulation. His practical education taught him empathy, compassion, and a general disdain for bureaucracy.

Doc's journey took him back to Canada where he worked in Saskatchewan for a while. He then moved his practice to Escanaba, Michigan. He was licensed in Michigan on July 9, 1929 and worked there four years. Licensed in Wisconsin in 1933, Doc moved with his wife Dorothy and son Edward Jr. to Washington Island in Wisconsin. This was during the Depression, and the Island guaranteed Doc $3000 a year; additionally, he sometimes received $1.00 for office visits and $3.00 for house calls. Doc dispensed medicine too, but like the visit charges, he often did not get cash for the medicines either. Bartering became the way of commerce. A chicken here, vegetables there, fresh venison quite often were some of the items Doc received in payment for his healing services. Doc loved the Island. Growing up on a Canadian farm, he had learned to love gardening, animals and hunting. He was a natural person with an outdoor bent, and the Island provided just the right mixture of nature, work and play. His wife, Dorothy, however, was not happy living on the Island. So, according to an article in the *Door County Advocate,* September 25, 1936.

Doc Farmer Doc Farmer Doc Farmer Doc Farmer Doc Farmer Doc Farmer Doc Farmer Doc Farmer Doc Farmer Doc Farmer Doc Farmer Doc Farmer Doc Farmer

20

"Dr. and Mrs. Farmer and son, Edward, left last week for Sturgeon Bay where they will make their home. Dr. Farmer will practice in that community."

Although Doc was disappointed about having to leave, the disappointment was double for the Islanders. In order to serve the Island, Doc made a trip to the Island once a week for appointments. He continued working in Door County for four years. During this period, Doc and Dorothy divorced and Doc met, soon to be second wife, Ruby Larson.

Ruby was born in 1910 and was the eldest of five children. She attended Carnot School in Southern Door County and graduated from Sturgeon Bay High School. She attended Bellin School of Nursing in Green Bay, Wisconsin and began working at the Sturgeon Bay Hospital. She and Doc skipped off to Holbrook, Arizona and married on July 10, 1940. Doc was thirty-six and Ruby was thirty. They were planning to live in Plainview, Texas, because that was stated in the Application for Reciprocal Endorsement by the Texas Board of Medical Examiners. However, they ended up in Grants, New Mexico, where they worked in a mission hospital. The State Board of Osteopathic Registration and Examination of New Mexico certificate, which gave Doc the right to practice in the New Mexico is dated May 31, 1939. The

State of New Mexico Certificate of proficiency in
Basic Sciences is dated March 2, 1940.

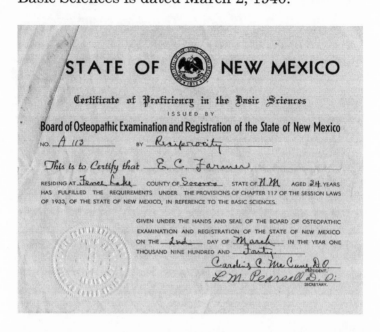

Ruby was a help-mate to Doc working in
a mission hospital in New Mexico, delivering
babies for indigenous people, and entertaining
friends like Hugh and Grace Black.

In an article dated April 11, 1941, in the
Door County Advocate, the following statements
occur:

*"A meeting was held at Nelson's hall Thursday
evening of last week to draw up a contract to present
to Dr. Farmer who might consider returning to the
Island. The Island has been without a resident doctor*

Doc Farmer Doc farmer Doc Farmer Doc farmer Doc Farmer Doc farmer Doc Farmer Doc farmer Doc Farmer Doc farmer Doc Farmer Doc farmer

22

since Dr. Little left for army service, except for the trips made here by Dr. Dorchester of Sturgeon Bay."

And an article dated, April 18, 1941, in the *Advocate* states,

"Town Chairman, Charles Hansen has received word from Dr. Farmer that the terms of the contract presented him as Island physician are satisfactory and that he will return here in June."

Maybe part of the decision to return to Wisconsin and the Island is that Ruby and Doc had just lost their first baby girl, Jewell Ida, in January 1941. She was born in Grants, New Mexico on January 7. Jewel Ida had a congenital heart problem and only lived a couple of days. What a blow to Doc and Ruby to be delivering healthy babies to others only to have their baby die.

Doc loved delivering healthy babies and 1500 of us (in Doc's guestimation) can thank our lucky stars and Doc for our delivery and some of the stories that follow.

Doc Farmer Doc farmer Doc Farmer Doc farmer Doc Farmer Doc farmer Doc Farmer Doc farmer Doc Farmer Doc farmer Doc Farmer Doc farmer

23

Doc with precious baby

Doc Farmer Doc farmer Doc Farmer Doc farmer Doc Farmer Doc farmer Doc Farmer Doc farmer Doc Farmer Doc farmer Doc Farmer Doc farmer

24

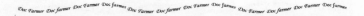

"In my inmost heart I believed that I could succeed where others failed, and now I had the opportunity to test myself."
                                    –Sherlock Holmes in 'The Musgrave Ritual'

Great Expectations

"My father delivered hundreds of babies," Jane Farmer Kane reminisces; "My mom, Ruby, who studied nursing at Bellin Hospital Nursing School in Green Bay, assisted. Some folks may wonder if delivering a child, when you have delivered hundreds, becomes a routine 'just another baby'. Dad would reply with an emphatic, 'No!'"

"Assisting a woman in the delivery of a child was always a special joy, especially if the arrival was a healthy normal child," Jane said.

"He always invited the husband/father to be present during delivery. He would say, 'you were there in the beginning, you will be there for delivery.'"

"When Dad and Mom worked at a Mission Hospital for indigenous people in Grants, New Mexico, from 1939-1941," Jane continues, "they would travel to humble homes of little more than one room and no electricity. Dad recounted how he delivered babies wearing a miner's hat with a light, and the older children would be lined up to watch."

That stint in New Mexico produced a lasting friendship between Hugh and Grace Black and Doc and Ruby Farmer—the kind of friendship that indelibly linked Grants, New Mexico, and Washington Island, Wisconsin and as you will see later in the book, kept a secret for fifty-nine years.

In June, Doc and Ruby moved to Washington Island.

One of the first babies Doc and Ruby delivered on the Island was to my parents, Maynard and Nora Gunnlaugsson. Lillian Mary was born August 28th, 1941. In those times, babies were delivered at home and because my mom and dad were living with dad's parents, Steena and Mac Gunnlaugsson, Lillian was delivered there. My mom tells it this way:

"Because Maynard, didn't want the neighbors to know what was going on (the telephone was on a party line)," Nora explains, "he went to get Doc Farmer and his wife Ruby to bring to the farm. It was 1:00 a.m. and Doc said the baby wouldn't be born until noon, but she was born at 6:00 a.m. During my pregnancy, I walked every day to Aunt Martha Gunnerson's because my in-laws would not allow me to do anything at their house. I think that is why my first delivery only took six hours. In those days, deliveries were natural, and I told Doc that I

Doc Farmer Doc farmer Doc Farmer Doc farmer Doc Farmer Doc farmer Doc Farmer Doc farmer Doc Farmer Doc farmer Doc Farmer Doc farmer

26

didn't think I could do it. He said, 'Yes, you can and you will!' Ruby in the meantime was pushing on my belly to help me deliver the baby.

"When Jeanie was born," Nora adds, "the bed broke (it was a brand new bedroom set). Doc was sitting on the bottom to deliver the baby, and Ruby was sitting at the top of the bed holding my hand, and it just collapsed. Jeanie was on her way, so Doc carried me into the smaller bedroom. He pulled the shade down, and it flew up and broke. 'What the hell else is going to happen?' Doc exclaimed. Jeanie was such a pudgy little bundle, I had a hard time having her."

(I, Martena, was the third child, the middle child, and I was born January 4, 1947 during one of the worst snowstorms of the winter. Dad had to keep plowing the lane in order to keep it open for Doc. I was born at 10:30 p.m. My parents now had three girls.)

So in 1950, when Nora was pregnant for a fourth time, Doc bet her a quarter that this would be a boy. She was going to name him Maynard Jr. but Doc delivered another girl, so she named her Maynette--as close to Maynard as she could get for a girl's name. Two weeks prior to the day Maynette was born, Nora started having pains. Doc came to check her and told her that the baby was ready to be born. Maynard was in Colorado, picking up a tractor for Ed Anderson's potato farm, and Nora had

Doc Farmer Doc farmer Doc Farmer Doc farmer Doc Farmer Doc farmer Doc Farmer Doc farmer Doc Farmer Doc farmer Doc Farmer Doc farmer

27

told him that she was not going to have the baby until he got back, and by golly she didn't. From then on Doc called her 'the stubborn Norwegian.'

Back: Lillian, Jeanie, Martena, Maynette, Kathy
Front: Nora, Maynard Jr.

In 1953, Doc delivered the fifth girl, Kathleen Amy. She survived because of Doc's intuitive doctoring. Maynard Jr. was born in 1960 when Doc was in Sister Bay. He was the only one of Maynard and Nora's children not delivered by Doc.

In those days, moms made up their own delivery pads to protect the bed. The pads consisted of two sheets sewn together with

Doc Farmer Doc Farmer Doc Farmer Doc Farmer Doc Farmer Doc Farmer Doc Farmer Doc Farmer Doc Farmer Doc Farmer Doc Farmer Doc Farmer

28

newspapers in between. Some of the women ironed them and put them in the oven. The afterbirth was wrapped in these pads and buried.

Doc was always good about coming to the homes as soon as he was notified that someone was in labor. Sometimes he just threw his coat on over his pajamas, if he had to rush.

Carolyn Koyen remembers one time Doc came rushing into their house in his pajamas and slippers. His slippers stuck to the floor because Alex had varnished some new kitchen linoleum, and it hadn't dried yet. She also remembers being late in her pregnancy and soon due to deliver. Doc told Alex (Carolyn's husband) that maybe a rough ride would help labor along so Alex put her into the cattle truck and took her on a rough ride through the gravel pit where their truck promptly became stuck. She said she would never forgive them (both Alex and Doc) for that little joy ride.

Doc's speed in an emergency was legendary. Carolyn Koyen recalls, "When Alex got attacked by the bull at Jack Hagen's farm, Doc was called. Clyde Koyen (Clyde's Garage) said Doc went by so fast, he was just a blurrrrrr."

Doc delivered babies in the family homes because there was no hospital on the Island. Later, Doc rented Carl and Pearl Haglund's home on Washington Island for delivering

Doc Farmer Doc farmer Doc Farmer Doc farmer Doc Farmer Doc farmer Doc Farmer Doc farmer Doc Farmer Doc farmer Doc Farmer Doc farmer

29

babies and for sick patient care. Pearl assisted him in the deliveries and took care of the babies and patients. If there was a problem, the patients would stay longer for extended care. In later years, babies were delivered in the home of Orville and Esther Wylie with Esther assisting Doc and caring for baby and mother.

Pearl Haglund's granddaughter, Kathy LeFavre, recalls:

"Doc Farmer was a part of our lives as he rented the Haglund house on McDonald Road for a time. He and my grandmother, Pearl, delivered many a baby there. My grandmother Pearl was a nurse with mid-wife training."

"My brother and I never knew where we would be sleeping at our grandmother's house. It all depended on who was having babies, or was sick, at the time of our arrival." Kathy goes on to say: "I even have the desk that was my great-grandmother's (Anna Haglund) upon which Dr. Farmer wrote many an instruction or prescription."

"Doc will always be part of our family's fond memories. As a young married woman, visiting my grandmother, Pearl, before an overseas assignment (my husband was with the military), I thought I had come down with the flu. No matter what my grandmother did to help, I still felt sick," Kathy relates. "So when my husband and I left, she called Dr. Farmer telling him we were on our way with

Doc Farmer Doc farmer Doc Farmer Doc farmer Doc Farmer Doc farmer Doc Farmer Doc farmer Doc Farmer Doc farmer Doc Farmer Doc farmer

30

instructions to stop in to have him take a look at me. We did stop and as Doc gave me the once over, he asked my husband if he had thought I had "caught" something? My husband just shrugged his shoulders, not understanding Doc's sense of humor. He had been referring to his feelings that I was pregnant, not sick with a flu bug. He gave me a shot of B vitamins and sent us on our way to Germany. By the time we reached the east coast I took time to have a pregnancy test at the military hospital in the area. Sure enough, ole Doc Farmer hit it right on the head—I was pregnant!"

"I know a lot of people still miss having him around. I know I do!" Kathy adds.

"Doc delivered all my babies," said Mary Jorgenson. "When I was pregnant with Paul, Walt (husband) and Dewey (brother) had gone up the road to Nelsons Hall (tavern) to shoot pool. Old Tom Nelson was in the habit of telling any wives that called for their husbands, 'No, he ain't here!' Walt had told Tom that if he got a call to come get him, but Tom forgot. When Mary called for Walt, several times, to tell him that she was in labor, and he needed to come take her to Esther Wylie's, Tom kept telling her Walt wasn't there.

Doc picked her up in his car and took her to Esther's. "I went in my slip," Mary adds. "Doc told me, 'well, you wear less than that at the beach.'"

Doc Farmer Doc farmer Doc Farmer Doc farmer Doc Farmer Doc farmer Doc Farmer Doc farmer Doc Farmer Doc farmer Doc Farmer Doc farmer Doc Farmer Doc farmer

31

Where was Walt through all this? He was happily playing pool. When Mary called again to tell Walt that Doc was taking her to Esther's, Tom said, "Oh, gosh dang it!" He finally remembered and told Walt that Mary was in labor.

Jewel Lee Hagen Grandy explains: "When I was due to be delivered, my Aunt Clarice, who was a nurse, was on the Island to help. She and mom had it all set up for me to be delivered at home in 'gasoline town' (a neighborhood on the north side of the Island). They had a hospital bed in the living room, and of course Grandmother Mamie was right next door. Mom stopped by to see Doc on the way to the Cherry Pie Festival and he said: 'You're not going to any festival; you're going home to have a baby.' And sure enough, he was right."

Shirley Atkins Ellefson remembers just getting out of Practical Nursing School. Doc and Ruby called to ask her to assist with the delivery of Myrtle and Chuck Goodlet's baby. "Oh God, no, I can't," Shirley remembers saying. "I was trained to take care of the patient after the delivery not during." But Doc convinced her, so Shirley helped deliver the baby. "Jimmy always says he is my baby whenever he sees me," Shirley laughs.

"Doc and Ruby delivered my first baby, Bruce, at Pearl Hagland's," Shirley continues. "It was a long labor and Doc used chloroform.

Doc Farmer Doc farmer Doc Farmer Doc farmer Doc Farmer Doc farmer Doc Farmer Doc farmer Doc Farmer Doc farmer Doc Farmer Doc farmer

32

When he said, 'Well, you had your little boy,' I said, "Why I did not! I didn't remember having a baby."

Bruce and Terry Atkins

"You couldn't help but like Doc Farmer," Shirley says. "You could call any hour, and he would come immediately. He did everything, and he was always good natured. People were not considerate of Doc's private time. He might be working in his garden, and someone would stop by just to have a blood pressure check. He would give advice over the phone, or anytime you wanted to see him, he made himself available."

Arbutus Greenfeldt said Doc only charged thirty-five dollars for pre and post-natal care in

Doc Farmer Doc farmer Doc Farmer Doc farmer Doc Farmer Doc farmer Doc Farmer Doc farmer Doc Farmer Doc farmer Doc Farmer Doc farmer

33

the 1940s. Office visits were two dollars, and there were no specified office hours. Doc was on duty all the time. "Both my and Harold's birthdays are on December 28," Arbutus explained.

"So when Susan was due about that date, we thought it would be great to have her on our birthday. Doc came down and induced labor. In the morning, he gave me castor oil. He came back in the afternoon and gave me something else. Susan was delivered at quarter to five. I had an awful time and pulled the bedpost out.

Later, after the delivery, Doc had to go to a Lions Club meeting, so Ruby stayed with me, and Doc came back about 9:00 p.m. to check on us and we were doing ok."

"When Betty Young was pregnant with, I think it was Ben," Arbutus said, "Doc had a dislocated knee. Betty had to get in bed with Doc so he could deliver the baby," Arbutus laughs. "He was unstoppable!"

Unstoppable and unflappable is a good way to describe Doc. Marcella Hagen had three difficult deliveries. Jack and Marcella's first born, Leila, said, "Doc saved my life. I was born at Esther Wylie's house and I was breech; I tore mom up something terrible. Mom was having problems as I was coming feet first, and Doc asked dad, 'Who do you want me to save, your wife or your baby?' Dad said, 'My wife!'

Doc Farmer Doc farmer Doc Farmer Doc farmer Doc Farmer Doc farmer Doc Farmer Doc farmer Doc Farmer Doc farmer Doc Farmer Doc farmer

34

When I finally was delivered," Leila goes on to say, "I was black from having the umbilical cord wrapped around my neck three times. Doc held me with his hands on my back and his thumbs on my chest squeezing and releasing to resuscitate me. All the time he was saying, 'Live! Live! Live!' He and dad took turns for about 45 minutes. A bunch of junk flew out of me and I survived. I always tell my students (Leila is a school teacher) the reason I can't spell is the blood was cut off from the spelling portion of my brain due to that umbilical cord.

Jack Hagen adds, "When Marcella was pregnant with our second child, Linda, and due any minute, Doc had to leave the Island to take Ruby to the hospital in Green Bay. There were three cars going to Green Bay: Doc and Ruby, Clyde and Gladys Koyen (Gladys had a broken leg), and Marcella and me. Doc said, 'If the baby is coming, honk, and I will stop and deliver in the car.' Four or five times we honked for Doc to stop, and all of us pulled over. When we got to the hospital, it was discovered that Linda lay sideways with her head in Marcella's hip socket.

The doctor at the hospital went in and turned her, and she delivered normally. Gladys Koyen always said she owned half of Linda for all the stops along the way."

"With Julian, our third baby, Jack continues, "Marcella had a normal delivery except she started hemorrhaging. Doc Farmer

Doc Farmer Doc farmer Doc Farmer Doc farmer Doc Farmer Doc farmer Doc Farmer Doc farmer Doc Farmer Doc farmer Doc Farmer Doc farmer

35

said Marcella had probably retained some of the placenta; I had to hold Marcella down because Doc was working her stomach so hard to get the rest of the placenta out.

Finally, Doc said, 'Oh, look at this piece of placenta.' And once that was out, Marcella stopped hemorrhaging. Because Marcella hemorrhaged so much, Doc told her, 'If they covered your face, Marcella, and I saw your stern, I would recognize you!'"

Doc induced a lot of babies. Sometimes it was because he was leaving the Island, sometimes it was because they were past due, and sometimes--as in Everall Jorgenson's case-- they were big babies.

Jorgenson's: (Back) Ted, Carla, Loretta, Wendy, Rex (Front) Everall and Chuck

Doc Farmer Doc farmer Doc Farmer Doc farmer Doc Farmer Doc farmer Doc Farmer Doc farmer Doc Farmer Doc farmer Doc Farmer Doc farmer

36

"Doc induced me with Loretta because he knew she was a big baby," Everall explains.

"She weighed 8 lbs 13 oz and each baby, after Loretta, got bigger. With Carla and Ted, I went into labor on my own. Wendy was big and Doc wanted to induce labor, but it was right around my sister Glenna's birthday. I didn't want her born on my sister's birthday. I wanted her to have a birthday of her own, but wouldn't you know, she was born on Glenna's birthday. Rex, the youngest, weighed in at 9 lbs 13 oz."

"Doc was with me for hours," Everall goes on to say. "He said, 'I'm really sorry; I am going to have to charge you $75 for the delivery.' After he got paid by the insurance company, he brought $25 back to us."

"Oh, my goodness! Only $50 to deliver a baby!" Everall exclaims.

"I remember the many times Doc came out to take care of my dad, Byron," Everall said. "He had asthma really bad. Doc would give him shots at 8:00 or 9:00 at night and then be called back out at 2:00 or 3:00 in the morning. Many, many times Doc never charged them for the visit."

LeVaun Mann Brown says, "If somebody couldn't pay, Doc would say just forget it, or he would take a chicken or vegetables in payment. He delivered three of my children—Bonnie, Jerry and Keith. All were delivered at Pearl Haglund's home.

Doc Farmer Doc farmer Doc Farmer Doc farmer Doc Farmer Doc farmer Doc Farmer Doc farmer Doc Farmer Doc farmer Doc Farmer Doc farmer

37

Ruth Gunnerson was delivered at Pearl's also; and Carl Haglund, Pearl's husband, had a hand in caring for newborns. Ruth recalls hearing that, "When it was time for me to be born, I was not coming as fast as Doc thought I should. He took Mom in his Model A on old bumpy back roads to induce labor. When I did come, I kept turning blue. The fifth time this happened, Carl Haglund grabbed me up and I started breathing again."

Daryl Justinger Johnson says, "Thinking of Doc Farmer brings only happy memories to mind of this dedicated, kind and thoughtful man. All four of our children were born on Washington Island and delivered by Doc. My husband, Don and I were living on the Island when our first daughter, Cheryl, was born in 1950. A few days after her due date, Doc told Don to take me on all the rough and bumpy roads he could find, but nothing happened. Doc then gave me a dose of castor oil, which I could not keep down, so again nothing happened. On Halloween day I spent the day at his home helping his wife, Ruby, with the laundry (to keep me active). By noontime, discomfort set in, and Doc kept a close eye on me until about 4:00 p.m. when he said it was time to go to the home of the mid-wife, Pearl Haglund. Timing the pains, he knew exactly when it was time to put the gown on and get me into the hospital bed. He then phoned for Don to come to Pearl's to see me before he gave me what I believe was ether to make the delivery easier. Cheryl was born about 7:00 p.m. and all went well.

New mothers usually stayed about one week at the mid-wife's home, and Dr. Farmer came each day to see the mother and baby.

"Four days later," Daryl goes on to say, "my girlfriend, Beverly Cook, came to Pearl's to have her first baby delivered. I was then moved to a cot in the dining room. Beverly's delivery was not as easy as mine, so it was very hard emotionally for me to bear the commotion in the delivery room. Then, Dr. Farmer came to me and asked if I would stand watch over the just born baby boy to check that he kept breathing because he, Pearl, and his wife, Ruby all needed to be by Beverly just then. I felt tremendous responsibility and became weak from it, but baby Gary was a trooper and did just fine!

We moved to Illinois a month later and when our next baby was soon due, my mother and father invited me to come back home and have Dr. Farmer deliver the baby. They would baby-sit Cheryl. Having the trust and confidence in our Island doctor made it sound like a great offer. So for our next three children, I always came back home to the Island and had Dr. Farmer deliver while mom and dad babysat. We have three daughters and one son. The doctor fee, I believe, was $50. The fee for our son's delivery was $5 more for circumcision."

"When I was a child," Daryl said, "I remember Dr. Farmer coming to our home to post a quarantine sign outside the door notifying anyone coming that there was a contagious disease inside the home. I do not ever remember Dr. Farmer not making a house call because of bad weather or bad roads. He always came through! And always with a smile and that laugh of his that we grew to love."

Joy Gunnlaugsson remembers Doc coming through when her first son, Jimmy, was born. "Doc had to go to Milwaukee," Joy recalls. "He didn't want to leave with me due any day. So he induced labor. He gave me castor oil in the morning, then shots until 10:00 p.m. Jim wasn't born until 12:00 a.m. but he was having trouble breathing, so Doc gave him a teaspoon full of Four Roses (whiskey). My husband, Russ, wasn't doing too well either, so my brother, Jack, took him outside and gave him a shot of Four Roses.

Esther Wylie put Jimmy in a basket and he started turning blue. She snapped the bottom of his feet to get him to start breathing again. Someone sat at his basket at all times. Evie Jessen, Esther, Ruby—all helped out. They devised a little oxygen mask and had a great big welding tank for the oxygen. I think it was ten to twelve days before he could breathe on his own."

Doc Farmer Doc farmer Doc Farmer Doc farmer Doc Farmer Doc farmer Doc Farmer Doc farmer Doc Farmer Doc farmer Doc Farmer Doc farmer

40

Russell Gunnlaugsson Family
Jim, Mack, Kirby, Joy and Russ

"With Kirby the cord was wrapped around his neck twice, but after Doc corrected that, there were no problems. Doc induced labor with my son, Mack, and he had breathing problems too, but it lasted only a few days," Joy adds. "In the year that Jim was born, there were twenty eight babies born on the Island."

In that year, 1948, Doc delivered, what an article dated July 22, 1948, in the *Door County Advocate* called, *"One of the state's smallest babies."*

Kay Katherine Koyen weighed in at 2 lbs 13 oz. She was born July 13. Her parents, Floyd and Gladys Koyen were ecstatic as they had lost a couple of babies before Kay's arrival.

"I was a twin," Kay Koyen Polster explains. "My sister did not survive. We were supposed to be born in September; but we arrived two months early. I was pretty small because when Margaret Smith made a sweater and bonnet for me, she used an orange for the bonnet's size. Even though I was small, I never had any problem with my lungs; in fact, I'm as healthy as a horse."

Doc Farmer did everything possible to help Kay survive. The *Advocate* article goes on to say: *"Little Kay did not have the advantages of a modern hospital with a convenient delivery room and a staff of nurses at her beck and call, but the local physician and his wife, Dr. and Mrs. E. C. Farmer, handled the delivery with efficiency and dispatch.*

...the quick thinking and ingenuity of Dr. Farmer and his wife (Ruby) overcame all obstacles."

Floyd and Doc built an incubator and when the thermometer didn't work, he used Ruby's candy thermometer. Several people recalled Kay's birth saying her head wasn't any larger than a teacup and she was kept warm with a light bulb and hot water bottle. Men's handkerchiefs were used for her diapers. Her bed was a shoebox with cotton in it.

Doc Farmer Doc farmer Doc Farmer Doc farmer Doc Farmer Doc farmer Doc Farmer Doc farmer Doc Farmer Doc farmer Doc Farmer Doc farmer

42

7/22/48

WASHINGTON ISLAND'S SMALLEST BABY, Kay Katherine Koyen, is shown having her diapers changed by Mrs. E. C. Farmer, wife of the physician who delivered the tiny tot last week Tuesday. The new arrival weighed 2 lbs. 13 oz. at birth.

A hand made incubator from the Door County Health Dept. is being used to bring the infant to normal weight, and the room is kept 80 to 90 degrees for times when Kay must be removed. The baby is a daughter of Mr. and Mrs. Floyd Koyen of the Island.

The Door County Memorial hospital cooperated by sending a special nurse who remained for the first three days.

The *Advocate* article continues:

"*Because the thermometer and oxygen tube occupy the opening through which the baby would normally be tended, the whole incubator top has to be raised in caring for little Kay. For that reason, the temperature in the room is held between 80 & 90 degrees by a coal burning cook stove. In this heat the doctor and nurse labored to keep the baby alive.*

Doc Farmer Doc farmer Doc Farmer Doc farmer Doc Farmer Doc farmer Doc Farmer Doc farmer Doc Farmer Doc farmer Doc Farmer Doc farmer

43

...Survival chances for such small premature babies are not high and had Kay been born before the Island had developed its unique medical cooperative system, she might not have survived. The population for Washington Island is not large enough to support a doctor by the usual fee system, so a system has been worked out whereby a cooperative group guarantees the doctor a minimum salary which is augmented by his practice fees.

This system is probably the most unusual in Wisconsin, but the Islanders have found from experience that it works satisfactorily to retain a doctor for this isolated place. For several years, the Island residents have been more than satisfied with their doctor and the system that brought him here."

Jane Farmer Kane remembers her dad talking about getting a call, in the early days on the Island, from a man who said his wife was going to have a baby. When he went to examine her, the lady told him, 'No man is going to look at me!' Doc said, "Well, how did you get into this situation?" She told him it was dark, and she was under the covers. So, Doc and the woman's husband went to the kitchen to have a cup of coffee. As they were leaving the room, Doc told her, 'When you need me, you'll call!' It wasn't too long and the woman was happy to have a man looking and assisting her."

Doc Farmer Doc farmer Doc Farmer Doc farmer Doc Farmer Doc farmer Doc Farmer Doc farmer Doc Farmer Doc farmer Doc Farmer Doc farmer

44

Doc became quite proficient in delivering babies, but he didn't have a stellar performance in predicting twins.

When Mary Richter went into labor in 1943, Doc didn't know she was going to have twins. 'He thought it was a big boy,' Mary told Lorna Bell Cornell.

"Mary was a small, slight woman, so in order for her to deliver Estelle and Adelle," Lorna adds, "Doc had to physically move the girls."

After the first one came, Arni Richter remembers Doc saying, "My God there's another!" After Estelle was born, Arni ran down to Pearl Haglunds to bring Pearl back to help deliver Adelle.

The same thing happened in 1947 when Grace and Raymond Jensen were having what they thought was their fourth child.

"Doc didn't know Mom was having twins," Eloise Jensen Curran said. "Eldon and I were seven weeks early when we were born January, 1947. When Mom went into labor, it was one of the worst snowstorms of the season. After Eldon was delivered at 5 lbs 5 oz, Doc said, 'Oh, wait! There's another baby coming!' He told dad to get some heat in the house. He wanted it 90 degrees—not just in the house but on the floor too. I weighed in at 5 lbs 1 oz, and Doc sent Dad to get baby supplies: 'Go to this one's house for that and that one's house for this,' he told him.

Doc Farmer Doc farmer Doc Farmer Doc farmer Doc Farmer Doc farmer Doc Farmer Doc farmer Doc Farmer Doc farmer Doc Farmer Doc farmer

45

Doc knew who had recent babies and might have baby things for the unexpected arrival of twins in the midst of a snowstorm."

To give Doc the benefit of the doubt, in the 40's there was not the sophisticated equipment and tests to determine the sex of the child or the number of babies a mom was carrying. It's common practice these days for doctors to use ultrasound to check the development of a fetus, to check the number of fetuses, and also to check for anomalies in the pregnancy. I wonder how many modern doctors, without their tests, would be able to determine if a woman were carrying twins.

Mildred Goodman Jacobsen didn't have twins, but Doc delivered all four of her children.

Goodman Family: Paul, Mildred, Matthew, Ruth, Norman

Doc Farmer Doc farmer Doc Farmer Doc farmer Doc Farmer Doc farmer Doc Farmer Doc farmer Doc Farmer Doc farmer Doc Farmer Doc farmer

46

Mildred said, "Doc could make you feel good just by walking in the door. When my last one, Norman, was born, Doc said, 'I thought when you had Norman for sure he would be named Edward. All these babies I've delivered, heh, heh, heh and not a single one named a child after me!'"

Doc got his wish later in Sister Bay with Phyllis and John Fitzgerald.

"I had seven girls," Phyllis explains. "After the last one, I told Doc that I would have to change doctors seeing he couldn't deliver a boy. When I was pregnant an eighth time, Doc came to deliver, and it was finally a boy, so we named him John, after my husband, and Edward, after Grandpa Norman and Doc. All three were pretty happy!"

Phyllis's second daughter, Kari Fitzgerald Brandt, in her book, *Seasons of a Farm Family*, adds to the family history:

...Kathleen Ann was delivered by Doc Farmer at the Sister Bay clinic. She was born January 2, and was the 1959 New Year's baby in Door County. ...In 1960, Mom gave birth to another girl (me), Kari Lynne. My shoulders were so big that Dad had to help Doc Farmer get me out. Grandpa Norman—who was thinking ahead—had already given Dad and Mom a gift for the baby. It was a baseball set, in obvious hope that the baby would be a boy.

Doc Farmer Doc farmer Doc Farmer Doc farmer Doc Farmer Doc farmer Doc Farmer Doc farmer Doc Farmer Doc farmer Doc Farmer Doc farmer

47

In 1961 Grandpa Norman—again hoping for a boy—bought a football for the next baby, but Doc Farmer delivered another girl, and they named her Jane Grace.... In 1963 Grandpa Norman—still hoping for that grandson—bought a basketball for the next baby, but Doc Farmer delivered another little girl; they named her Julie Susan.

In 1965 Grandpa Norman—not giving up hope—bought another baseball set for the next baby, but Doc Farmer delivered yet another girl. Mom and Dad named her Connie Lee.

In May of 1970—during my birthday party—our old farmhouse caught on fire. ...Mom was seven months pregnant at the time, and was so upset that Doc Farmer was called to be with her. ...In July, Mom was ready to have her baby, and Grandpa Norman—still believing for a boy—bought another football. But once again Doc Farmer delivered a baby girl; they named her Carol Jeanette. Long-time friend and neighbor, Jeff Weborg, who then worked for Dad, asked if he was disappointed because he didn't get a boy. Dad replied jokingly, "No, that's okay; it just means I'll have to try again."

In 1972 Doc Farmer delivered the last Fitzgerald girl at his Sister Bay Clinic; she was given the name Jackie Lynn. This time——thinking that they'd never have a boy—Grandpa Norman brought no sports equipment for the new arrival.

Doc Farmer Doc farmer Doc Farmer Doc farmer Doc Farmer Doc farmer Doc Farmer Doc farmer Doc Farmer Doc farmer Doc Farmer Doc farmer

48

In October of 1976, however, the "retired" Doc Farmer was called to the Fitzgerald farm and with the help of wife, Margaret, and Dad—who did indeed 'try again'—finally delivered their baby boy. He was of course named John (after his father) Edward (after the joyfully proud Grandpa Norman, and ever helpful Doc Farmer).

People couldn't get over how many children my parents had; occasionally someone would even comment. With a twinkle in his eye, Dad would respond, "After a while it's just like spittin," to which Mom would roll her eyes and reply, "Right John; it would be a little different if you were doing the spittin'!"

'Spittin'. Only a man could describe having a baby as 'just like spittin'.

Lawrence Housman once said, "If nature had arranged that husbands and wives should have children alternatively, there would never be more than three in a family." Now, there is a man who knows what it's all about.

Virginia Johnson was happy Doc knew what delivering babies was all about. She said, "My son, Kerry, was brought into this world by Dr. Farmer at his clinic, November 9, 1957, at midnight. I was home with the baby at 8:00 p.m. the next day. His clinic was located at that time in a building a bit south of Bunda's Store on Hwy 42 in Sister Bay. I had a very healthy boy,

Doc Farmer Doc farmer Doc Farmer Doc farmer Doc Farmer Doc farmer Doc Farmer Doc farmer Doc Farmer Doc farmer Doc Farmer Doc farmer

49

and his well being was well attended to after his birth by Dr. Farmer. Yes, Dr. Farmer was a wonderful doctor. His likeness, I'm sure, is not to be found these days. I'm sure he was as important to Washington Island as he was to Sister and Ellison Bay. Memorialized he should be."

Cathy Gibson Jorgenson missed having Doc on Washington Island when she was pregnant with Tammy. Dr. Pinney was the doctor on the Island then, and when he started having his problems, Cathy decided to go off the Island to Doc Farmer in Sister Bay. When she went into labor, they had a special ferry to take her and Perry to the mainland. They stayed right at Doc and Ruby's home. Every couple of hours Ruby would give her another shot 'to help the labor along.' That evening, after Tammy was born, Perry and Cathy were sleeping downstairs. Doc and Ruby slept upstairs.

"Tammy fussed all night long," Cathy said. "We tried everything to get her to go to sleep but nothing worked. Doc had told us to come get him if there was any problem, but we hated to disturb his much needed rest. Finally, we thought maybe there was something wrong with the baby, so Perry went upstairs to wake Doc. Doc jiggled, jiggled, and jiggled Tammy until she burped and passed a little gas, and she calmed right down. Doc was always there for you," Cathy added.

Doc Farmer Doc farmer Doc Farmer Doc farmer Doc Farmer Doc farmer Doc Farmer Doc farmer Doc Farmer Doc farmer Doc Farmer Doc farmer

50

Cathy's sister Doreen had a similar experience as told by her sister-in-law Angie Gauger (in Fish Creek). "When the stork decides, it arrives, whether there is a doctor or not. This was the case for my brother Everett and his wife Doreen. They lived on Washington Island and Dr. Pinney was gone. Doc Farmer's practice was in Sister Bay at that time. It was a very blustery March night, and they made a fast call to the ferry line. The ferry had to buck ice all the way to the mainland. About 12:30 or 1:00 a.m., I got a call from Doc, and he said the baby wouldn't arrive for a while and did I have room to put them up. The next day Doc kept calling to see how she felt and how far apart the contractions were. The time finally arrived, and she went to Sister Bay and had a nice baby girl named Candis Ann. This is the only time I got to give a baby its first bath," Angie said.

Delivering babies and watching them grow up was a source of pride for Doc. Ruth Gunnerson tells it this way:

"I was at Ruth Goodman Weiting's wedding in Menominee Falls, Wisconsin, sitting next to Doc Farmer. At an appropriate time, Doc poked me in the side to get my attention and with a broad smile on his face, said, 'Twenty seven of you I brought into this world.' Then he chuckled.

Not many doctors can look around a church sanctuary more than 200 miles away

Doc Farmer Doc farmer Doc Farmer Doc farmer Doc Farmer Doc farmer Doc Farmer Doc farmer Doc Farmer Doc farmer Doc Farmer Doc farmer

51

from where his practice was and recognize each of his deliveries many years later. Of course, the bride was included in the count."

"Dad delivered babies for 40-some years in his practice," Jane Farmer Kane explains, "only discontinuing when it became necessary to purchase malpractice insurance."

"The insurance was very expensive, and Dad only charged around $100 for prenatal care and delivery. A baby boy's circumcision was a few dollars more. He did not want to raise his prices to cover the cost of insurance."

Doc did not keep a record of all his deliveries so we can't add them up for a full count but if he guestimated 1500, it's probably a pretty reliable count.

It had to be providential that in 1923 when Doc entered The Chicago College of Osteopathy, the laws changed so Doctors of Osteopathy could legally practice obstetrics. Thank goodness and providence.

Doc Farmer Doc farmer Doc Farmer Doc farmer Doc Farmer Doc farmer Doc Farmer Doc farmer Doc Farmer Doc farmer Doc Farmer Doc farmer

52

"Let us get a firm grip of the very little we do know, so that when fresh facts arise we may be ready to fit them in their place."
— Sherlock Holmes in' The Adventures of the Devil's Foot'

The Fifty-Nine Year Secret

If solving the mysteries of illness is a major part of doctoring, then keeping secrets is a close second. The ethical questions invading Doc's life, the privacy rules surrounding the Farmer family, and the decisions to 'let sleeping dogs lie' must have caused many sleepless nights for a man who relished honesty.

Because the Doctor's office was at the Farmer home, Jane Farmer Kane said she and her sister learned at an early age that what they heard at the house stayed at the house.

"My sister and I were taught at a young age how to answer the phone with 'Dr. Farmer's, just a moment please.' As we grew, we learned how to take a message, name, phone number and time of call. We also were taught that whatever we might hear from phone conversations or patients talking with Dad, that it was no one else's business. For example, if we overheard that someone was going to have a baby, it was not our business to announce it to anyone."

Doc Farmer Doc farmer Doc Farmer Doc farmer Doc Farmer Doc farmer Doc Farmer Doc farmer Doc Farmer Doc farmer Doc Farmer Doc farmer

53

"It was a strict rule," Jane said, "never repeat anything you hear!"

Farmer home as it appears today on Washington Island

"Doc was very good at keeping privacy," Andrea Tischler Lundquist (Doc's medical technician) explains. "He didn't chart everything out."

Hannes Andersen of Washington Island remembers (in the 40's) a young girl who went to work for a farmer. She got pregnant and the child was born at home. Her mother took the

Doc Farmer Doc farmer Doc Farmer Doc farmer Doc Farmer Doc farmer Doc Farmer Doc farmer Doc Farmer Doc farmer Doc Farmer Doc farmer

54

baby out to the outhouse and threw it down the hole of the toilet. The daughter started bleeding. Doc Farmer was called and said, 'Where's the baby?' They said, 'there's no baby.' Doc said, 'Don't try to fool me, that's post partum bleeding if I ever saw it!'

"No one was ever prosecuted," Hannes stated emphatically.

Right or wrong -- ethical decisions were a part of Doc's everyday life. In the forties, the social stigma that went along with unwed motherhood drove many families to desperate measures. Unwed mothers were often considered living in sin and were often forced to give their children up for adoption. Doc was instrumental in one such adoption and went to his grave with the keys to a major secret.

Marianna Hanson Gibson knew she was adopted. Her adoptive parents, Art and Bernice Hanson, were open about her adoption. She knew she was delivered by Dr. Farmer. She even knew the name of her biological mother, Philena Black. She knew her mother was from Grants, New Mexico. What she didn't know filled her head with questions for 59 years: Why was she given up for adoption? Who was her father? What were the health issues? Why did someone from Grants, New Mexico come all the way to Washington Island, Wisconsin to have her baby?

Doc Farmer Doc farmer Doc Farmer Doc farmer Doc Farmer Doc farmer Doc Farmer Doc farmer Doc Farmer Doc farmer Doc Farmer Doc farmer

55

Marianna grew up on Washington Island as Art and Bernice's only child. She was well cared for, especially by her dad, Art, but she longed for brothers and sisters. She longed for a big family, so when she and Herb Gibson married in 1971, they set about fulfilling her wish. First came Anita, then Frank, Art, Becca, Anna and Sarah. Since Herb and Marianna owned the West Harbor Resort, the large family was a big help in taking care of the nine rooms in the main lodge and the six cottages. Running an Inn and raising six children, Marianna didn't have much time to delve into her past. When two of their children turned up with hazel eyes, they thought that was curious, but that wasn't enough to prompt an investigation of the adoption records. However, when son, Frank, was diagnosed with epilepsy, Marianna became serious about researching her family history.

But where to begin?

"I went to the courthouse," Marianna said, "and the lady was very rude but she gave me a pamphlet on the Wisconsin Adoption Search Agency. So I read the flyer and contacted them. The lady was very nice, and said she could print the information but without the names in it, because my mother was dead. That was the first I learned that Philena had died in 1997. But if I wanted names in it, I had to get a court order."

Doc Farmer Doc farmer Doc Farmer Doc farmer Doc Farmer Doc farmer Doc Farmer Doc farmer Doc Farmer Doc farmer Doc Farmer Doc farmer

56

In the meantime, it just so happens that Herb and Marianna's oldest daughter, Anita, was house sitting in Santa Fe, New Mexico.

Because Grants, New Mexico, wasn't too far from Santa Fe, she decided to take a little side trip to research the "Black" family. The place to begin, she decided was the library. Anita didn't hold out much hope for coming up with something specific or even anyone who knew the Blacks, so she was amazed when the woman at the library not only knew of them but had gone to school with Stephanie--Philena and John Matkovich's daughter. And if Anita would like to speak with Stephanie, she was part owner in a restaurant just down the street.

Anita was in a dilemma. Should she spill the beans about Marianna? What repercussions would that bring? She decided she would just go talk with Stephanie as a customer and mention a family connection to the Blacks. Anita found her very easy to talk with and found out that Stephanie's mom, Philena, and her dad, John, were both deceased and that she had a brother and sister. Anita called her mom. Marianna thought she needed to get more information to be able to prove she was part of the family. So Anita didn't tell Stephanie anything about her mother. However, before she left Grants, New Mexico, Anita got Stephanie's address.

Marianna goes on to explain: "I had contacted the Wisconsin Adoption Search

Doc Farmer Doc farmer Doc Farmer Doc farmer Doc Farmer Doc farmer Doc Farmer Doc farmer Doc Farmer Doc farmer Doc Farmer Doc farmer

57

Agency in the summer of 2006, but being our busiest time, the research about my adoption records was put on the back burner. I figured I had to hire an attorney to get a court order. So I didn't get around to talking to Jay Ward until December. He is an attorney who had stayed at the Inn with us, and he and his wife built a home on the Island, which they moved into permanently when Jay retired. I told him what I wanted, and he said that he used to work with adoptions when he first became an attorney. I gave him the information I had. A judge can say no to signing a court order and then you can't get the records open, so Jay researched it.

Seeing my mom was dead, I was the only one who could get the records open. Because I had good cause, wanting to research my family medical history, the judge signed the court order the end of February. So in March, the lady from the Wisconsin Adoption Search Agency called me. She said she didn't print the information again, as I already had it without the names and it would cost more money. I told her to print the information with the names in it because I needed to prove who I was. They might think I was just talking through my hat.

This is the information Marianna received:

Adoptive Investigation
July 21-22, 1948

Doc Farmer Doc farmer Doc Farmer Doc farmer Doc Farmer Doc farmer Doc Farmer Doc farmer Doc Farmer Doc farmer Doc Farmer Doc farmer

58

Re: Petition for the Adoption of
Marianna Black by Arthur Hanson
and Bernice Hanson

"Dr. Farmer stated that the baby was a full term baby, weighing 6 pounds at birth. The delivery was normal. The child was bottle fed from birth. She has had no illness to date and was 16 ½ pounds in July.

The baby was seen several times by worker and appears to be an unusually alert baby, smiles easily at visitors and entertains herself in the crib. The Hansons have been very faithful in following the doctor's advice as to feeding and training and the child's physical condition shows the results of good care. Child has reddish blonde hair, blue eyes and is very fair skinned."

Natural Parents
Paternity

"Paternity was not established for this child. The father is a single man living in New Mexico. Philena and this young man were planning to marry but broke off the relationship. He was still writing to her when she lived at the Farmers. It seemed that he was not willing to marry Philena immediately but did write to her. Philena was very much hurt and emotionally upset, the Farmer's advised, and felt that Philena would not go back to this man.

Philena Black was born August 12, 1928, at Grants, Valencia County, New Mexico. She is a daughter of Mr. and Mrs. Hugh Black, who still reside in Grants. Philena is of English and German ancestry. She has only one sister, older than Philena, recently married and expecting a child. Philena completed grade and high school including commercial training

Doc Farmer Doc Farmer Doc Farmer Doc Farmer Doc Farmer Doc Farmer Doc Farmer Doc Farmer Doc Farmer Doc Farmer Doc Farmer Doc Farmer Doc Farmer

59

and was hired to work as a typist for an insurance company in Grants. She worked there until she became pregnant. She returned to the job after the confinement.

Both the petitioners (for adoption, Art and Bernice Hanson) and Dr. Farmer stated that Philena appears to be an intelligent girl, very attractive and according to Dr. Farmer, in excellent health.

Dr. Farmer stated he knew the family health history and he knew of no instances of feeble-mindedness, insanity, or epilepsy. He stated all of the family are in good health.

Consent of the mother, properly signed before the County Judge, was secured from Philena before she left the county and is on file with the petition."

In a letter written by the Door County Public Welfare Department to Miss Mary Weaver (Consultant of Adoption Division of Child Welfare) in Madison, Wisconsin it is stated:

"In investigating the placement I found that Philena had promised the Hansons the child before the confinement since her parents would not permit her to take the baby home. The Hansons were eager to adopt a child but took the precaution of going to New Mexico to check on Philena's background. They visited her family, Mr. and Mrs. Hugh Black, and found they were respectable people in good circumstances and of good social standing, and that there is no unfavorable health history within their family or in that of the alleged father."

"I found Dr. E.C. Farmer who attended the birth very cooperative in giving information on the unmarried mother and the circumstances of placement. He, at one time, lived and practiced near the Black family and knew them well. Philena planned to marry the alleged father but apparently the man changed his mind and refused to marry her. Philena then wrote Dr. Farmer to see whether she could come to Washington Island to have the baby. The Farmers said they would be glad to have her come and even offered to have her stay with them indefinitely and work for them if she wished to keep the baby herself. Philena, however, did not want to stay in Wisconsin and, therefore decided to place the child with Mrs. Farmer's sister and brother-in-law, who had no children but before Marianna was born, the prospective adoptive mother became pregnant. The Hansons heard of this and asked if they could take the child. Fortunately, the Hansons are a very fine young couple and everyone contacted recommended them very highly. They have never applied to an agency for a child and still hope to have children of their own in addition to this child.

The social worker goes on to say,

"I also took this opportunity to ask Dr. Farmer to report all illegitimate pregnancies or births as promptly as possible to the Division of Child Welfare or to our office since there is no hospital or maternity home on the Island, so that the unmarried mother may be assisted in plans for herself and her child without so much delay. He advised he would be glad to cooperate.

…I do not know if you will recommend another contact. However, if so, Dr. Farmer felt we should warn the investigating agency to consider all information very confidential and to make contacts in such a way that no embarrassment would be caused the Blacks, who evidently feel Philena's situation a family disgrace."

In a way, Marianna felt some relief after reading the information. It seemed her mother

Doc Farmer Doc farmer Doc Farmer Doc farmer Doc Farmer Doc farmer Doc Farmer Doc farmer Doc Farmer Doc farmer Doc Farmer Doc farmer

61

was forced into giving her up. Her grandparents would not permit Philena to bring the baby home because in 1948 this would disgrace the family. Philena's boyfriend, Marianna's father, washed his hands of the whole affair. Philena had to make the big decisions on her own. Bless the Farmers for offering their home and work as an option; after all, they had just had a baby girl, Jane, in January, a month and eleven days prior to Marianna's birth. Philena, at 19, decided, what she considered, best for the baby—to provide a loving home. But how could Philena leave her baby after carrying her for nine months, delivering her on a distant Island and taking care of her for a month before returning to New Mexico?

"It wasn't because you weren't loved!" These were the words Marianna wanted to hear more than anything else in the world. But she would never hear them from her mother; she had already died.

More questions haunted Marianna's mind. Would her sisters and brother want to know they had an older sister? Was their father her father? What response, if any would she get? And the big questions: Would she still be a disgrace to the family? Was she a big secret still?

What happened next is one of those 'its time has come' situations:

Doc Farmer Doc farmer Doc Farmer Doc farmer Doc Farmer Doc farmer Doc Farmer Doc farmer Doc Farmer Doc farmer Doc Farmer Doc farmer

62

"I didn't quite know how to begin a letter to Stephanie," Marianna explains, "Here I had all this information but didn't know how it would be received fifty-nine years after the fact."

This is the letter Marianna wrote:

March 6, 2007

Dear Stephanie,

 I'm not quite sure how to start this letter so here goes.

  Last January, my oldest daughter, Anita, talked to you about a family connection to the Black family. I thank you for taking the time to talk to her. She said you were very kind to her and easy to talk to so I thought you would be the one to write to. My husband and children have encouraged me to look into my family history so I contacted the Wisconsin Adoption Search Agency. I have enclosed some of the information received from them. I guess you could say finding my birth parents has been a thought of mine for many years but I was afraid to pursue it until now. There always seemed to be a blank spot when I would talk about my life.

  I am awed by the information I received about my mother and father. I do feel sad that it won't be possible to meet them. I knew my mother had lived on Washington Island some months before I was born and that her name was Philena Black. As I grew up on the Island, there were a number of people that told

Doc Farmer Doc farmer Doc Farmer Doc farmer Doc Farmer Doc farmer Doc Farmer Doc farmer Doc Farmer Doc farmer Doc Farmer Doc farmer

63

me I look like my mother. I was and am curious if I really do—I have blonde hair and blue eyes too. I do have a baby necklace (an Indian design) my mother sent me for my first Christmas.

After graduating from High School, I went to college for 3 ½ years, married my husband, Herb, in 1971, and we are blessed with six children. They are Anita, 35, Frank 30, Art 28, Becca (Rebecca) 27, Anna 24 and Sarah 19. We own our own business— Gibson's West Harbor Resort. It is really a family business and busy in the summer and kind of quiet in the winter.

When I was growing up I always wanted brothers and sisters and to realize I do have some is a dream come true. I don't know if you had any idea about another sister and apologize for the shock if you had no idea. I would love to meet you, Susan, and Stephen if you would give me the opportunity—I know this is asking a lot.

I would love to hear from you. (Here Marianna added her address, telephone numbers and e-mail)

Thank you for reading my letter,
Love, Marianna

What Marianna didn't know is that she sent the letter addressed to Stephanie to Stephen's address. The letter was sent in a

Doc Farmer Doc farmer Doc Farmer Doc farmer Doc Farmer Doc farmer Doc Farmer Doc farmer Doc Farmer Doc farmer Doc Farmer Doc farmer

64

Gibson's Resort envelope. It could have just been another advertisement. Luckily, Stephen was out of town and guess who was taking care of his house and picking up the mail?? Stephanie. When Stephanie received the letter, she couldn't believe it was true. She had never heard anything about her parents having another baby and this baby was only three years older than her older sister, Sue. She talked to Stephen and they decided to call Marianna.

"On March 12, 2007, I was at Bethel Builders," Marianna explains. "I picked up my cell phone and there was Stephen's number; he had tried to call me. I was so excited, but also nervous at the same time. I called Anita and told her, she said, 'Well, call them!' When I did, Stephen and Stephanie were so excited to think they had another sister. They knew nothing about Washington Island or about me."

In April, Marianna and Herb flew to New Mexico, so Marianna could meet her sisters Sue and Stephanie and her brother Stephen. With the information from the Wisconsin Adoption search agency, Marianna and her sisters and brother knew John was Marianna's father too.

Here were the sisters and brother Marianna had wished for all her life. They were able to fill in some of the pieces missing from Marianna's story. Philena did end up marrying her boyfriend, John, a year and four months after Marianna's birth. John's parents were very

Doc Farmer Doc farmer Doc Farmer Doc farmer Doc Farmer Doc farmer Doc Farmer Doc farmer Doc Farmer Doc farmer Doc Farmer Doc farmer

65

strict and they probably never knew about Marianna. As far as they could determine, no one knew except Philena, her boyfriend John, her parents, her sister Elsie, and Washington Island.

"It was fun filling in the blanks in my life," Marianna said. "I found out I am like my mom in many ways. She collected everything — buttons, bows, wrapping paper; she sewed; she did crossword puzzles; and she was very active in her community, the things I like to do. And the mystery of the hazel eyes: "My dad had hazel eyes."

But best of all were the words Stephanie said to Marianna: "It wasn't because you weren't loved that you were given up. Mom loved children. She was a very good mom."

"I believe how she handled leaving me on Washington Island," Marianna concludes, "is Doc Farmer kept her informed as I grew up.

Stephen remembers a letter from Doc stating, 'Marianna is doing well.' He thought nothing of it, but I think, maybe that is how she got by. I think there was an understanding between Philena and my adoptive parents that she would have no contact with me."

"I wouldn't be up here on Washington Island, if it wasn't for Doc Farmer," Marianna said. "As you can tell, Doc had a lot to do with my adoption."

Bless you Doc!

L to R: Marianna Gibson, brother Steve and sisters Sue
and Stephanie

Doc Farmer Doc farmer Doc Farmer Doc farmer Doc Farmer Doc farmer Doc Farmer Doc farmer Doc Farmer Doc farmer Doc Farmer Doc farmer

67

"I have never known anyone so vitally alive. He lived intensely—every fibre of him!"--Mary Maberly to Sherlock Holmes in 'The Adventure of the Three Gables'

Tough Bugger

'Tough bugger'--this is what Dick Bjarnarson called Doc Farmer. But after you read Dick's story, you may question who actually is the 'tough bugger.'

"It was March 3, 1946," Dick begins. "I was 13 years old and hunting crows with John Gunnlaugsson and David Foss. David was at the other end of the woods, so he wasn't there when the accident occurred.

I was hunting with a model 97 Winchester pump shotgun. This model had been known to go off even with the safety on. (After it was all over my dad and I walked back to where it happened. I let the gun drop off the stump with the safety on, and the same thing happened.)

We weren't even moving when the accident occurred. I was just standing on a stump, leaning on the gun. It slid off the stump, the hammer knocked through the safety and the way I was leaning the shot went through my arm. We quick rushed toward the house, it just so happened as we were nearing the end of the

Doc Farmer Doc farmer Doc Farmer Doc farmer Doc Farmer Doc farmer Doc Farmer Doc farmer Doc Farmer Doc farmer Doc Farmer Doc farmer

68

road that Dad (Oliver) was getting out of his truck. When we hollered that I had been shot, he started running toward me.

"No! No! Go call the doctor!" I hollered.

Dad went back to the house and called Doc Farmer, and then he came back to get me. I was losing a lot of blood. By the time we got back to the house, Doc Farmer had gotten there. He cut my jacket and sleeve off and made a tourniquet out of an inner tube. He took a stick and twisted the tourniquet to stop the bleeding. It hurt worse than being shot because my skin was twisted up in the tourniquet.

Doc called for airplanes from Sturgeon Bay, Wisconsin and Escanaba, Michigan. These airplanes were small two-seaters. We needed three—one for me and Doc, one for mom and one for dad. Wally Arnson from Escanaba sent over two airplanes. George Meredith from Sturgeon Bay made it first because he had a tailwind. Doc and I got in with George, and we took off from the ice in Detroit Harbor. We got over Rock Island and the carburetor on the airplane started freezing up. We had to make an emergency landing on the ice.

In the meantime, the two airplanes arrived from Escanaba. One picked up my mom (Esther) and the other one picked up my dad. The plan was to fly to the hospital in Escanaba, Michigan. The plane that picked up mom had passed us already and didn't see us make the

Doc Farmer Doc Farmer Doc Farmer Doc Farmer Doc Farmer Doc Farmer Doc Farmer Doc Farmer Doc Farmer Doc Farmer Doc Farmer Doc Farmer

69

emergency landing. The one that picked up my dad saw us go down on the ice, so they landed on the ice too. They transferred me and Doc to Wally Arnson's plane, and when we taxied down the ice and turned into the wind, the airplane went through the ice. It was held up by the struts. They forced the door open, slid me out and told me to roll. Of course, when I rolled, the tourniquet came lose. Blood was squirting up in the air. Jimmy Cornell caught me on the ice and held me down. I think I kind of passed out because I had lost so much blood. They ended up taking me to Doc Farmer's office.

They called Dr. Dan Dorchester, who used to fly his own plane, and he flew up. I needed a blood transfusion. The only one they knew on the Island who had my blood type was Doc's sister-in-law, Doris Hettiger. She was not supposed to give blood because she had asthma so bad. She demanded they take it. I ended up with 1 ½ pints of her blood.

Dr. Dorchester and Dr. Farmer amputated the arm two inches above the elbow. They couldn't save the elbow because there were too many BB's in it. The fine shot in the gun was #6 fine shot. I still have BB's behind my ear, one in my breast and some in the stump.

In the meantime, my mother was stuck over in Escanaba, Michigan. She couldn't get back until the next day. I hardly recognized her when she came in. She looked like she had

Doc Farmer Doc farmer Doc Farmer Doc farmer Doc Farmer Doc farmer Doc Farmer Doc farmer Doc Farmer Doc farmer Doc Farmer Doc farmer

70

turned gray overnight. Luckily, Dad was on the Island with me.

I stayed at Doc Farmer's office, which was in his home, for three days. I had to have penicillin shots every three hours. Doc and his wife Ruby took shifts giving me the shot. They were nice people. After a couple of days they had a little party for me. They had the high school kids come down, and they served pop and ice cream.

After three days I went home. That was alright until one time about two weeks later I went out with Georgie Mann and my grandfather Waldemer. We were in the woods skidding logs. I drove the John Deere tractor to skid the logs off. I loved driving tractor. That night when I got home, my right hand seemed to be squeezing. They took me down to Doc Farmer and he said, "There isn't anything I can do for you. You just have to block that out of your head." It was just the nerves from the jiggling of the tractor that had upset things.

Doc Farmer was a wonderful man, a tough bugger. He could pull teeth. He took my tonsils out with just a local. He could do most anything. He was the only shot we had up here. Everything seemed to come natural. Doc did a beautiful job sewing my arm up.

Doc Farmer Doc farmer Doc Farmer Doc farmer Doc Farmer Doc farmer Doc Farmer Doc farmer Doc Farmer Doc farmer Doc Farmer Doc farmer

71

Dick Bjarnarson

Doc Farmer Doc farmer Doc Farmer Doc farmer Doc Farmer Doc farmer Doc Farmer Doc farmer Doc Farmer Doc farmer Doc Farmer Doc farmer

72

"A dog reflects the family life. Whoever saw a frisky dog in a gloomy family or a sad dog in a happy one? Snarling people have snarling dogs, dangerous people have dangerous ones. And the passing moods may reflect the passing moods of others."

     ----Sherlock Holmes in 'The Adventure of the Creeping Man'

Frisky Dog

     Doc loved animals. While living on the Island, he had two boxers called Jezebel and Zonnie. Mary Jo Richter Purinton remembers Jezebel lying on Bill Smith's corner as if she owned the whole area. Most people remember Zonnie. Joy Gunnlaugsson remembers being at Doc's office and Zonnie wanting to go outside. Seeing no one was letting him out, Zonnie went right through the screen.

     Herb Gibson and Cathy Gibson Jorgenson remember their dad Frank almost cutting his finger off while chopping wood. While Doc was stitching up Frank's finger, Zonnie was sitting anxiously nearby. Doc said, 'Oh don't mind Zonnie, he thinks I'm taking out tonsils and expects me to throw him a set.'

     Cathy also remembers the special treatment Doc gave their cocker spaniel Tinker. "One day we were out for a drive; Tinker jumped out of the window and rolled down Jack Hagen's hill. We kids were so upset we rushed her to Doc

Doc Farmer Doc farmer Doc Farmer Doc farmer Doc Farmer Doc farmer Doc Farmer Doc farmer Doc Farmer Doc farmer Doc Farmer Doc farmer

73

Farmer. He took her ever so gently and talked to her the whole time he was looking her over. 'She'll be just fine,' Doc pronounced with his heh, heh, heh reassuring laugh."

Grace Kopitzke Rossman recalls Doc saving their cocker spaniel Midnight:

"In the summer of 1963, my twin brother and I were walking to the beach along highway 42 with our cocker spaniel Midnight. Somehow, she found herself tangling with a motorcycle. Dog and bike both ended up in the ditch. Midnight was in bad shape—she was bleeding everywhere and had severe abdominal injuries.

We ran home and got Dad, who arrived on the scene with his huge Pontiac and a sheet of cardboard. He slid the cardboard under Midnight. The motorcycle driver and Dad lifted the dog into the trunk. I rode with Dad, and we hightailed it to Sister Bay and Doc Farmer's clinic. Doc stopped everything and helped Dad carry Midnight in through the back where he did surgery on the dog right then and there. Dad served as his surgical assistant. That crazy dog recovered completely, and she lived another seven years after that. I have no idea if there was a vet in the area at the time, but I'm sure Midnight never saw one."

Ray Cordon was very grateful to Doc for helping in an emergency situation with their dog, Shatzie.

Doc Farmer Doc Farmer Doc Farmer Doc Farmer Doc Farmer Doc Farmer Doc Farmer Doc Farmer Doc Farmer Doc Farmer Doc Farmer Doc Farmer

74

"One beautiful summer day, my wife Connie, my daughter Helen, me and our standard schnauzer Shatzie, were enjoying the day on our lawn in Ellison Bay. Shatzie was off her lead, ran onto the road and was hit by a car.

I was in shock and didn't know what to do. Connie and Helen took Shatzie up the road to Doc Farmer's house. I believe it was a Saturday or Sunday. They told Doc they knew he was a people doctor but could he, please, take a look at Shatzie. Doc told them she was bruised over her body but it was not visible because of her thick coat. She would heal naturally. Shatzie would whimper at night, from the pain, but she did heal up in a short time. We were very grateful to Doc for helping in our emergency."

John Mueller remembers his dad, Dr. Clarence Mueller, his grandfather, Dr. Beard, and Doc Farmer removing the scent glands from a skunk. They all ended up smelling like skunk when they were done but John thought it was cool. He was sure he would be the envy of all his friends when he brought that skunk home to Illinois with him.

Jane Farmer Kane had a pet skunk too. "A mother skunk was hit by a car and left three little 'kits.' Dad removed their scent glands (working outside); he later had to bury the clothes he had worn for the procedure. We kept one kit and found homes for the other two."

Doc Farmer Doc farmer Doc Farmer Doc farmer Doc Farmer Doc farmer Doc Farmer Doc farmer Doc Farmer Doc farmer Doc Farmer Doc farmer

75

Jane laughs remembering: "It was summer, visitors from the city would come to our house asking for the doctor. When my sister or I would answer the door we would have the little skunk on our shoulder to greet folks! Wish I could describe the looks of surprise and all the emotions that flashed on their faces."

One of those pet skunks was given to Renee Glos-Block. She said, "I was born on Washington Island, August 15, 1949, delivered by Doc Farmer at Esther Wiley's confinement home. My dad always told me he didn't have the money to pay for my delivery because they were just starting the resort, 'The West Wind' in West Harbor. He told me Dr. Farmer agreed on 10 lbs of fish to deliver me. My dad said he, Doc, and my godfather, Dave Lucke, were all at the kitchen table downing shots of bourbon and I cost 10 lbs of fish.

As I grew up, every time I got in trouble, my dad would say to me, 'I should have kept the fish!!'

Dr. Farmer also gave me my first raccoon and my first 'defumed' skunk for pets. He was a very, very eloquent and special man."

Doc took the name 'Farmer' to heart. He kept chickens, turkeys, and whatever animal he was given in payment for his services—even a lamb from which they ended up enjoying 'the harvest of the meat.'

Doc Farmer Doc Farmer Doc Farmer Doc Farmer Doc Farmer Doc Farmer Doc Farmer Doc Farmer Doc Farmer Doc Farmer Doc Farmer Doc Farmer

76

Jane remembers a rescued hawk. "The hawk was injured and couldn't fly. We kept it in the small animal's quarters. It eventually healed and was released."

Even snakes were not contraband. Doc let it be known that he would pay to have snakes delivered to his home in Sister Bay to keep the rodent population down.

There wasn't a vet on the Island, but Steve Gunnlaugsson was the man to call if an animal was having problems. In Hannes Andersen's book, *Washington Island Through the Years*, Hannes Andersen states:

"Steve Gunnlaugsson, The Animal Doctor, was self-taught and had an excellent understanding of animal's ailments and how to treat them."

Steve's son, Cliff, remembers Steve and Doc consulting on many cases.

"He would ask Doc for advice," Cliff said. "At many a birthday party celebration I remember dad and Doc sitting together going over the doctor book.

Ken Falk remembers when he was young one of their milk cows stepped on her udder. His dad, Gilbert, called Doc. He doesn't remember what Doc told his dad, but that milk cow turned out just fine.

Doc Farmer Doc farmer Doc Farmer Doc farmer Doc Farmer Doc farmer Doc Farmer Doc farmer Doc Farmer Doc farmer Doc Farmer Doc farmer

77

Jim Anderson remembers one animal Doc wasn't especially fond of—crows. The Island was overrun with crows while Doc was township Chairman. They were eating all the farmers' crops and Doc's garden.

"When Doc was Island Chairman," Jim said, "they were paying $.15 a crow, so I used to try anything to get a crow. That was a lot of money back then. I remember ringing Doc's doorbell, holding up the dead crow, and Doc digging in his pocket for $.15 and saying, "Got another one, eh Jim?"

Doc even had his daughter, Jane, bring him worms. "My first job, that I remember, was to find cut worms in the garden and to collect them into a can in early summer," Jane explains. "Later in the summer, it was to collect cabbage worms in a can. I received a penny a worm."

Of course, Doc didn't keep the worms for pets but his garden surely thrived, and Jane learned the value of a worm.

Animals, be it human or otherwise, were in good hands when cared for by farmer Doc.

Doc Farmer Doc farmer Doc Farmer Doc farmer Doc Farmer Doc farmer Doc Farmer Doc farmer Doc Farmer Doc farmer Doc Farmer Doc farmer

78

"I guess most men have a little private reserve of their own in some corner of their souls where they don't welcome intruders."
  --Sherlock Holmes in 'The Problem of Thor Bridge'

Lions Club

Doc was instrumental in starting several Lions Clubs in Door County. "Unselfish service to others" being at the heart of the Lions Club and Doc, the two seemed a very good fit. We can only speculate how Doc originally heard about the Lions. Jack Hagen thinks maybe Doc became acquainted with the Lions when he was going to school in Chicago. That is a very good possibility because the Lions Club was formed in Chicago, June 17, 1917, by Chicago businessman, Melvin Jones. According to the Lions Club International website, the club was a dream of Melvin Jones, who "believed local business clubs should expand horizons from purely professional concerns to the betterment of their communities" and this betterment involved "building parks, assisting youth, awarding scholarships, providing help in time of disasters, vision and health screening and support of eye hospitals."

But it also could be that Doc became a part of the Lions Club because of his younger sister Martha. According to Jane Farmer Kane,

Doc Farmer Doc farmer Doc Farmer Doc farmer Doc Farmer Doc farmer Doc Farmer Doc farmer Doc Farmer Doc farmer Doc Farmer Doc farmer

79

"Dad's sister had crossed eyes. She was about 12 years old when Dad went off to medical school. Dad made arrangements for her to see a specialist in Chicago. It turned out she was too old for the specialist to do anything about her vision problem but Martha always appreciated her big brother for trying to help."

The Lions Club is very much involved in vision screenings, collecting eyeglasses and 'known for working to end preventable blindness.' In fact, in 1925, Helen Keller spoke at their international convention in Ohio and challenged the Lions to become "Knights of the blind in the crusade against darkness." I could picture Doc taking that challenge to heart and therefore helping to start or participate in every Lions Club in every community in which he lived.

The Washington Island Lions Club was formed in 1934. In an article in the *Door County Advocate* dated 14 June 1935 the headlines read, Island Lions Club Will Get Charter:

"The local Lions Club, which was organized last winter and which has grown into a thriving organization doing considerable public service, will be presented with its charter by the Rev. J Richard Olson of Milwaukee, present district governor, tomorrow evening at a banquet that will be attended by a large delegation of Lions from Sturgeon Bay and other points....Officers of the local club are Ernie Boucsien,

Doc Farmer Doc farmer Doc Farmer Doc farmer Doc Farmer Doc farmer Doc Farmer Doc farmer Doc Farmer Doc farmer Doc Farmer Doc farmer

80

president; Roger Cornell, first vice-president; William Hansen, second vice-president; William Smith, third vice-president; Dr. Edward Farmer, secretary; Fred Dillon, tail twister; and Jens Sorenson, lion tamer."

Doc sponsored many into the Lions Club. Pete Oleson said, "Doc was a super recruiter." One of Doc's recruits was Ray Hansen and he has been a Lion for 50 years.

Steve Gunnlaugsson was an early Lion as told by Hannes Andersen in his book, *Washington Island Through the Years*, Hannes Andersen said:

"He (Steve Gunnlaugsson) was one of the first members of the Lion's Club when it was organized in the mid-thirties. Meetings were usually held at James and Martha Sorenson's West Harbor resort where a delicious meal could always be expected. In those days the Lion's demanded more participation at meetings by all members. One assignment for the next meeting was to make up a poem about the member sitting to your right. This was to be presented at the next meeting. It so happened that Steve was sitting on brother Marvin's right. Marvin tried desperately to create a suitable poem about Steve. Finally, with my assistance, this was accomplished."

Maybe writing poetry wasn't for everyone in the Lions Club but the Island high school

Doc Farmer Doc farmer Doc Farmer Doc farmer Doc Farmer Doc farmer Doc Farmer Doc farmer Doc Farmer Doc farmer Doc Farmer Doc farmer

81

teacher, L. A. Davison, loved to write poetry so it would be no surprise that he contributed his fair share. Doc received the 'Lion of the Year' award in 1955 on the Island. A poem written by L. A. Davison sums Doc up quite well:

What's been a secret, deep and dark
Has finally come to light.
Who is the Lion of the Year
Is hot news here tonight.

We've waited patiently to hear
Which Lion it would be.
We couldn't quite be certain, but
We guessed it would be he.

He is a man of varied parts.
Whatever task's at hand
He does with eagerness and zeal
For Washington Island.

As hunter, also gardener,
He stands in high repute,
And as a politician he
Is said to be astute.

Doc Farmer Doc farmer Doc Farmer Doc farmer Doc Farmer Doc farmer Doc Farmer Doc farmer Doc Farmer Doc farmer Doc Farmer Doc farmer

82

But Doctoring's where he excels...
    He's really tops at this.
Though Island bound the year around
    He never is remiss.

He'll feed a hypochondriac
    A pink or yellow pill,
But slave from morn 'till night for one
    Of us who's really ill.

His diagnoses are correct
    From pregnancy to gout,
And usually his treatments cure...
    He knows what he's about.

He is a very busy man...
    On call around the clock,
A common, unassuming guy,
    To all of us, he's "Doc".

"Doc" Farmer, Lion of the year,
    Man of integrity,
No finer choice could have been made!
    On this, we all agree.

                                L. A. Davison

Doc Farmer Doc farmer Doc Farmer Doc farmer Doc Farmer Doc farmer Doc Farmer Doc farmer Doc Farmer Doc farmer Doc Farmer Doc farmer

83

On July 29, 1975, Washington Island honored Doc with a presentation of a lion statuette inscribed with recognition of his services to the Island community.

Doc receiving his Lion Club award from Percy Johnson

How Doc found time in his busy schedule, one will never know except to say when it came to service, Doc took on the Lion's share.

Doc Farmer Doc farmer Doc Farmer Doc farmer Doc Farmer Doc farmer Doc Farmer Doc farmer Doc Farmer Doc farmer Doc Farmer Doc farmer

84

"Holmes had read carefully the note which the last post had brought him. Then, with the dry chuckle which was his nearest approach to a laugh, he tossed it over to me."

--Watson in 'The Adventure of the Sussex Vampire'

The Case of the Leaking Window

Doc Farmer had a wonderful sense of humor. He knew that laughter was the best medicine so he tried to fit a joke in every chance he got. Because I was only 10 when he left the Island, I never heard any of his off color jokes. He saved those for his grown-up patients and friends but, as you will see, this was probably one of his best true life tales:

Sunset Resort is a well-known and very well-liked hotel on Washington Island. It is family owned and family run. If you want a great breakfast, you'll find it at Sunset Resort and you can't beat the view of the setting sun. Back when Lois Hagen and Maxine Engstrom were running the resort, the rooms did not have their own private bathrooms. In order to let the fresh Island air in the rooms, the windows were propped open with a stick.

Ok, so put a man in a room without a rest room. Put a stick in a window holding it open.

Doc Farmer Doc farmer Doc Farmer Doc farmer Doc Farmer Doc farmer Doc Farmer Doc farmer Doc Farmer Doc farmer Doc Farmer Doc farmer

85

Imagine what would happen if he had to go to the bathroom really bad. Option 1, rush down the hall to take the chance the restroom is unoccupied. Option 2, wet the bed. Option 3, (now remember this is a male) use the open window as the urinal.

Can you guess what happened next?? Why would Maxine and Lois have to drive the poor fellow to see Doc Farmer? What happens to boys who make their own rest rooms? And what ever happened to the stick?

Lois and Maxine did not go in to Doc's office with the man. They thought he might be reluctant to relate the whole story but as they sat in the car waiting for the man to come back out, the only thing they could hear was Doc's hardy laugh-heh, heh, heh—echoing through the house.

So the moral of the story is don't trust a stick propping open a window and beware of leaking windows.

"Doc laughed everyday," Andrea Lundquist (Doc's medical assistant) relates.

"I never saw him angry. I was young and innocent when I worked at the clinic. Doc tried not to tell his jokes when I was around. All those old guys were so adorable."

Jane said of her dad, "Any topic or subject, Dad had a joke. While he was in college, he didn't have much money, so for a wedding

Doc Farmer Doc farmer Doc Farmer Doc farmer Doc Farmer Doc farmer Doc Farmer Doc farmer Doc Farmer Doc farmer Doc Farmer Doc farmer

86

gift for his younger sister, he blew up a bunch of condoms and put them in a pretty box."

If he had a full blown sense of humor he also had a quiet subtle way about him. Jane said, "I only remember Dad yelling at me twice. Once when I brought the car home with an empty gas tank and once when I came in late about 2:00 am.

He told me, 'Jane, a girl doesn't get in trouble with too much moonlight, but a girl can get in trouble with too much beer.'"

Carol Richter Lemon remembers one night when Doc temporarily lost his sense of humor. It was Halloween evening and the goblins were out and about. This was in the days of outdoor toilets. Because outhouses had to be moved every once in a while, they were very seldom bolted down, and they were prime targets for tricksters. Two particular trick-or-treaters were out that night and just happened to see Doc go into his outhouse. As he settled in for a little read, they snuck up behind that potty and "Push! Push! Push!" they screamed in unison. Over went the potty, all those Sears' catalogs, and Doc.

"It just so happens, we pushed it over on the door so Doc couldn't get out," Carol recounts the story. "As we were running away, all we could hear was Doc screaming, 'If I live to be 100, I'll get you Carol Richter and Diane Stelter.' He obviously recognized our voices

Doc Farmer Doc Farmer Doc Farmer Doc Farmer Doc Farmer Doc Farmer Doc Farmer Doc Farmer Doc Farmer Doc Farmer Doc Farmer Doc Farmer

87

when we were hollering push. I don't know how he got out. We were long gone by then.

Good thing he didn't live to be 100 because I don't remember him getting us for that little prank," Carol adds.

Maybe because Doc loved a good joke, he let this little trick go. Maybe he thought if he could dish it out, he'd better be able to take it.

Dr. March said of Doc, "He was a practical joker. He told a lot of off-color jokes--he liked teasing people."

For once, Doc, the embarrassment, so to speak, was on you.

In *Door Way*, Norbert Blei writes:

"One joke, though, leads to another, and no man alive knows and tells more jokes than Old Doc Farmer. The only trouble is, most of them are unprintable. But they do work wondrous cures for his patients and friends.

... 'That's like the one about the two old ladies...'and he's off again, I'm convinced some of his best patients fake an illness just to stop in the office and hear Doc tell a new story.

... "If you can get a patient to smile, they don't feel so depressed. You have to be able to laugh at yourself. So I always like to tell them a good joke."

Now whether my father's, (Maynard's) favorite joke was dispensed by Doc, I don't know

Doc Farmer Doc farmer Doc Farmer Doc farmer Doc Farmer Doc farmer Doc Farmer Doc farmer Doc Farmer Doc farmer Doc Farmer Doc farmer

88

but it might express the lighter side of his humor. It goes like this:

A man and his son set up the new railroad track and train the boy had gotten for Christmas. After everything was put together and the train was rolling down the track, the dad passed some gas (my dad would say, 'let out a doozy'). The dad said to the son, 'Did you hear the whistle?' The son replies, 'No but I `mell the `moke'.

If dad didn't get this `little doozy` joke from Doc then I am sure he told it to him several times because he would tell and retell that joke and laugh harder with each retelling.

Chief Oshkosh, Doc, and Maynard Gunnlaugsson

Doc Farmer Doc farmer Doc Farmer Doc farmer Doc Farmer Doc farmer Doc Farmer Doc farmer Doc Farmer Doc farmer Doc Farmer Doc farmer

89

"The example of patient suffering is in itself the most precious of all lessons to an impatient world."

--Sherlock Holmes in 'The Adventure of the Veiled Lodger'

Keeping in Stitches

Doc Farmer kept everyone in stitches, not only with his jokes, but with his needle and thread. Being a rural country doctor, he never knew what the day's harvest would bring to his door.

Grace Sowa had a harrowing experience when she and husband, Albert, set out on their honeymoon.

"I met Dr. Farmer on a scary day in the summer of 1959. Albert and I had set out on our honeymoon from Chicago's Monroe Harbor, in June, in an old 27 ft. Seabird yawl. One of our destinations was Ellison Bay in Door County, Wisconsin, where Albert's uncle was vacationing with his family.

We limped into the harbor in August. We had broken the centerboard in a storm on the way. Albert and his uncle purchased 8 ft. sheets of plywood, which they screwed together. By diving under the boat, they hoped to slide the makeshift centerboard into its slot, which came through the cabin floor. I was to guide it from inside with ropes, watching through the slot. It

Doc Farmer Doc farmer Doc Farmer Doc farmer Doc Farmer Doc farmer Doc Farmer Doc farmer Doc Farmer Doc farmer Doc Farmer Doc farmer

90

was a hard job getting the board pushed down into the water, and it wanted to jam in the slot.

None of us expected what happened next. I was hovering over the slot. Albert and his uncle were under the water, pushing and shoving—repeatedly having to come up for air. We had almost given up when the board aligned and shot into the cabin, with my forehead the only thing in the way. I was a bloody spectacle. Albert thought I had lost an eye."

They rushed to see the county's doctor, Doc Farmer.

"Dr. Farmer inspired confidence right away. He was kind and gentle, and he sewed up what turned out to be a gash along my eyebrow. He didn't shave off that eyebrow, for which I am still grateful, and he readily agreed that Albert's aunt could remove the stitches. The charge was $5 probably $35 in today's money.

Years later, our friend, Jim Kane, Albert's fellow teacher, married Jane Farmer. One day she mentioned she was from Sister Bay in Door County, and that her father had been the doctor there. We've had fun with that story ever since. Six degrees of separation? Probably only one or two if you talk long enough."

Talking was one of Roger Gunnerson's strong suits. He enjoyed a good meal and conversation over any type of pain as his daughter, Ruth, relates:

"Papa was doing one of his marathon runs (as we called them) where he left the Island on the first boat in the morning with a load to take down to Waukesha, Wisconsin. He got there, unloaded, and headed back north. He stopped in Baileys Harbor to mow the lawn for Grandpa Rosengren. Being tired, he bent down to pick up something in the way and ended up cutting off three of his fingers. He wrapped the ends of the fingers in one handkerchief, his hand in another and finished mowing the lawn. After finishing the lawn, he headed up to Doc Farmer's house in Sister Bay. Doc was having dinner so Papa joined to talk, keeping his hand in his pocket. Dinner was finished and Doc turned to Papa and said, 'Well, Rog, what can I do for you?' At this time, Papa showed him the fingers and his hand.

Doc said, 'Time is important with these sorts of things; why didn't you tell me instead of waiting for us to finish dinner?'

Papa said he had finished the lawn and waited this long, so he was sure a few more minutes would not matter. Doc got a fifth of whiskey out, and they each had a shot. He then began sewing the three fingers back. By the time they were done, they had finished the whiskey. All three fingers healed, joining back with only part of one nail being truly lost."

For her own experience of Doc's handiwork, Ruth said,

Doc Farmer Doc farmer Doc Farmer Doc farmer Doc Farmer Doc farmer Doc Farmer Doc farmer Doc Farmer Doc farmer Doc Farmer Doc farmer

92

"At about age six, on Island Fair day, I was running in the yard and ended up stepping on a Spam can. I got a deep 'S' shaped cut on my big toe. Mom washed it out and wrapped it to stop the bleeding. Papa took me over to Doc Farmer to sew it up. Those were seven stitches that I was able to show off for a long time. Then when I was about ten, Doc Farmer pierced my ears. He had a piercing gun to shoot pointed gold posts through the dots he made to mark the spots. No pain, no ice cubes, no potatoes and no problems."

Injuries of any kind were not for this mother, Everall Jorgenson:

"When Carla cut her finger, I wrapped it in a towel," explains Everall. "Chuck was working in the gravel pit so instead of running Carla to Doc, I ran to Chuck and then, together, we took her to see Doc. I sat out in the car, crying, while Chuck took Carla in. A few minutes later, Ruby, came out to the car and said,

'You should be ashamed of yourself! Here your daughter is sitting in there being a big girl and you are out in this car crying.'

"I just couldn't stand to see the sight of blood. Luckily none of my kids had any broken bones. I don't know what I would have done," Everall adds.

Michael Flood worked with Doc Farmer at Nor-Door Clinic in Sister Bay. He was a

Doc Farmer Doc farmer Doc Farmer Doc farmer Doc Farmer Doc farmer Doc Farmer Doc farmer Doc Farmer Doc farmer Doc Farmer Doc farmer

93

physician's assistant/nurse practitioner. He said, "Dr. Farmer was very good at suturing. A young girl came in. She had fallen on a fence and cut off her long finger at the distal joint and she was quite worried about it. I told Doc we probably ought to get her to a hand surgeon. 'No,' Doc said, 'I've done a lot of these myself.'

He was very busy that day, as was I. So I proceeded to soak the end of her finger in a bucket of saline water and anesthetized it. The distal end of her finger was quite traumatized so Dr. Farmer did sew it on, put a dressing on and it did well. She came back in ten days to have the sutures removed and the nail was on the palmar aspect of the hand, not the dorsal aspect, which meant Doc had sewed the finger tip on wrong, but it worked; so he simply took the fingernail off and cauterized it. She now has a fingerprint on the back of her long finger and a scar on the palm side of her joint but the joint looks good and it healed quite normally."

"He was quite a remarkable man," Mike goes on to say. "He did a lot by the seat of his pants. He was very knowledgeable and he knew when to refer and not to refer. I learned a lot about practical medicine and that empathy was the better part of sympathy. We miss him. He worked all of his life and left nothing. But as he used to say to me, 'You cannot take anything with you anyhow, so it does not make any

Doc Farmer Doc farmer Doc Farmer Doc farmer Doc Farmer Doc farmer Doc Farmer Doc farmer Doc Farmer Doc farmer Doc Farmer Doc farmer

94

difference. Just do what the good Lord lets you do.'

Another favorite expression of Doc's was, 'Waste not, want not.' Working through the depression and having to provide all the supplies, Doc would not waste anything, as Mike relates:

"My first day at the clinic, July 5, 1976, a patient came in with a laceration to her hand, and I went to suture her up. I talked to Dr. Farmer, asked him where all of his Betadine and suture material was, as I was not familiar with the office. He showed me this little emergency room which was a 10x10 square room with some cabinets and a table. He told the patient to sit down in the chair and proceeded to tell me that he did not use Betadine, he just used Ivory soap and water because it cleaned just as well, which was acceptable to me. I also asked about the suture set-up, asked him where the suture material was, and he said to go to that pan over there. I went over to the silver pan where he had a needle holder with a needle on it and about half the suture material was gone already. Then I asked him where the new needle holder, the new sterilized drape sheets and the new suture material was. He said for that particular suture put in only 3-4 stitches and that was all I needed for this cut, so just use that one. I found it kind of hard to swallow having been new at

Doc Farmer Doc farmer Doc Farmer Doc farmer Doc Farmer Doc farmer Doc Farmer Doc farmer Doc Farmer Doc farmer Doc Farmer Doc farmer

95

microbiology and pathophysiology, just out of school. At that time, there was no indication of any known diseases such as HIV, hepatitis B, hepatitis C, etc. We did suture the patient up. The patient did well with someone else's suture and needle. However, I told him the next time, I would like to order some new suture material, get a new sterilizer, and individual suture material so we did not have to use that again."

Greg Casperson remembers playing basketball and tearing his leg up. Doc didn't use any anesthetic; he just poured whiskey on the wound and told Greg to take a swig. It required 25 stitches.

You had to be tough to go to Doc. He expected a stiff upper lip. Skin tags (those pesky little bits of skin hanging by a peduncle) were one thing you didn't mention to Doc or he might just snatch them off as he did to Winfield Anderson as told by Bruce:

"Dad went to see Doc at home and he had a skin tag on his temple. Doc said, 'Come on out behind the woodshed' and he yanked it off. 'You're going to bleed a little but you will be fine,' Doc told him."

Jane Farmer Kane's husband, Jim, was working on some shingles on the roof and hit his thumb with a hammer. "The nail was about ready to come off, when Dad and Margaret came to visit," Jane explains. Dad said, 'Let me have a look at that.' As Jim was showing him, Dad

Doc Farmer Doc farmer Doc Farmer Doc farmer Doc Farmer Doc farmer Doc Farmer Doc farmer Doc Farmer Doc farmer Doc Farmer Doc farmer

96

ripped the damaged nail off, saying, 'let me take care of that!' 'See', Dad said, 'now the new nail has room to grow.'"

Carol Richter Lemon said, "Doc was one of a kind. I was jumping on mom and dad's bed and cracked my skull open on the baseboard. Doc shaved my head, poured a shot of whiskey on it, saying, 'you'll forget this pain.' He took a mallet and pounded a metal clamp in. I never remembered the pain."

Steve Eaton laughs, "I was always afraid of Doc. Whenever I had to go see him my mom would say, 'heh, heh, heh, time to go see Doc.' But, I was afraid of everything, so you can't go by me."

Mack Gunnlaugsson remembers a couple times he went to see Doc.

"One time I can remember standing on a table at Doc's with my pants down around my ankles with a four inch needle stuck in my a-- and him saying, 'this won't hurt a bit, heh, heh, heh.'

The other time, Mack had gotten a metal sliver in his eye. "Dad took me down to Sister Bay where Doc had his office. He crawled up on my chest and was using a needle to dig the sliver out."

Eric Greenfelt remembers when he was eight or nine years old that Doc sewed up his hand:

Doc Farmer Doc farmer Doc Farmer Doc farmer Doc Farmer Doc farmer Doc Farmer Doc farmer Doc Farmer Doc farmer Doc Farmer Doc farmer

97

"I was playing with a gallon jug (pottery) of water. As I was climbing the hill, I slipped, the jug broke on the rocks, and I cut my wrist. We put a bandage on the bloody mess and went to see Doc. He sewed it up, and I never had any problems. It healed great."

Shirley Atkins Ellefson recalls Doc sewing up her son's cheek after he was hit with a swing. Terry had a scar on his cheek, but it wasn't because of Doc's lack of finesse.

"Before it ever healed," Shirley sighs, "Terry was standing on a chair. He fell off and opened it up again. The scar wasn't Doc's fault."

Tonsillectomies were an important part of Doc's 'preventive medicine' procedures. These were the days when antibiotics were not readily available, and sore throats and tonsillitis were common occurrences. The tonsils were supposed to take an active part in the immune system support but often times, they became a breeding and holding ground for infections. Doc got so good at tonsillectomies that he could 'peel them out like a grape'.

I remember when I had my tonsils taken out about the age of five or six. I was put to sleep. I remember being wrapped like a mummy, lying on Doc's table and Ruby administering that awful smelling ether. I know I fought her, tooth and tonsil. Jane said her mother, Ruby, was very nervous about giving ether. It could cause burns so she carefully

Doc Farmer Doc farmer Doc Farmer Doc farmer Doc Farmer Doc farmer Doc Farmer Doc farmer Doc Farmer Doc farmer Doc Farmer Doc farmer

98

spread cold cream on the face to protect the skin before she had to administer just the right amount. It was one of the hardest things she had to do.

For me, although I fought it, I am glad he put me out. I think he did this for all children but if you were an adult or close to an adult, he only gave a local. My mom, Nora, remembers Doc taking her tonsils out and gagging when Doc accidentally dropped them back into her throat. She told him he'd better get them all out because she certainly wasn't coming back for another try.

Jim Anderson remembers Doc taking his tonsils out. "I thought he was trying to kill me!" Jim confesses. "Ruby was trying to put the mask over my face for the ether and I fought it all the way." (Jim probably thought Doc was trying to get him back for all the times he rang Doc's doorbell and then ran).

Tonsillectomies often became a family affair. Sylvia Landin remembers all three of her daughters--Arlene, Darlene and Joan--having their tonsils removed at the same time. She had to go upstairs and lie down. There's only so much a mother can take.

Mary Richter fainted when Doc worked on all four of the girls.

"I was first," Carol Richter Lemon recalls, "I was about eight or nine years old. I was awake through the procedure." Estelle, Adelle and Mary Jo came next. The instruments weren't real sterile. Ruby was shaking them and wiping them on her white uniform. Afterwards, we were given ice cream shakes. When we left, mom carried Mary Jo and I carried the twins, one in each arm across the street to our house."

Carol also remembers a friend of hers who lived in Sister Bay, "He cut his hand while working for Masterfreeze Corporation. He went to Doc and it required quite a few stitches so Doc gave him two fingers of bourbon to numb the pain. That was a staple in his 'medicinals' to control pain."

Arni Richter didn't have his tonsils out at the same time, but he remembers he wasn't put to sleep when Doc removed his tonsils. Arni grimaces, "I remember lying on that kitchen table and I felt it!"

Dick Bjarnarson said he just had a local—maybe it was Novocain--when he had his tonsils removed. Doc stuck a tongue depressor down his throat and removed the tonsils. "I gagged a little, but Doc did a beautiful job sewing me up." Dick said, "He could pull teeth; he could do most anything."

Jack Cornell went to Doc's office to have a tooth pulled because there was not a dentist on the Island.

"Here I am in the chair," Jack relates, "Doc puts his knee up on my chest and pulls my tooth--just like that!"

A similar thing happened to Walt Jorgenson as told by his wife, Mary.

"Walt went to Doc with a toothache, and Doc said, 'Is this the tooth?' Walt said, 'Yep'. Doc jumped on his chest. Walt was so surprised, he jerked back and the tooth popped out."

Jack Hagen recalls Doc pulling about ten of his upper teeth.

"He loved to pull teeth," Jack relates. "One tooth of mine, Doc pulled and pulled and finally got it out but he broke a root, and it caused massive infection. I ended up going to a dentist in Kewaunee and he x-rayed my jaw and found that root fastened to my sinus. He pulled it out and no more infections."

Herb Gibson remembers the time he and his sister had teeth growing outside other teeth. "Doc pulled the ones underneath," Herb explains. "He expected you to be tough."

Cathy Gibson Jorgenson remembers their sister, Darlene, having teeth pulled.

"Doc used chloroform and told Darlene, 'Oh, you'll never remember a thing.' But Darlene remembered! Cathy stated emphatically, "She never forgot!"

Larry Young never has forgotten when he was about six years old wrestling with his brother, Bob. "I ended up with a broken leg," Larry laughs. "I remember Doc using his x-ray machine in his basement, using plaster of paris

Doc Farmer Doc farmer Doc Farmer Doc farmer Doc Farmer Doc farmer Doc Farmer Doc farmer Doc Farmer Doc farmer Doc Farmer Doc farmer

101

for the cast and then cutting that cast off with a little buzz saw."

Marty Jacobs remembers, "Back in the early seventies, the head of the family dropped a wrench on his head when working on the roof of the house. The cut on his head was pretty big so we drove him up to Dr. Farmer's house. We were met by a barking dog, and Doctor in his bathrobe since it was nine in the evening. The Doctor washed the cut at the kitchen sink, shaved some hair off with a razor, brought out his black bag and stitched him up. Doc told him to have someone in the family take the stitches out in a week and charged him $7.00."

From sewing to sculpting, Doc kept practicing his healing arts, calming words, reassuring ways and natural remedies. He was a Doc for all seasons.

Doc Farmer Doc farmer Doc Farmer Doc farmer Doc Farmer Doc farmer Doc Farmer Doc farmer Doc Farmer Doc farmer Doc Farmer Doc farmer

102

"Possibly you have heard of his reputation as a shooter of big game. It would indeed be a triumphant ending to his excellent sporting record if he added me to his bag."

–Sherlock Holmes in 'The Adventure of the Mazarin Stone'

Man for All Seasons

Although it seems a contradiction to Doc's nature, hunting, especially deer hunting, was an outlet for Doc. He hunted with my dad, Maynard, as well as other Islanders and other Door County folk like Chief Oshkosh. Hunting was one of the reasons he loved Door County. Doc grew up hunting with his father and brothers in Canada so his love of hunting carried over into adulthood.

"He was a good shot," Cliff Gunnlaugsson recalls. "In later years he preferred taking shots with his camera rather than his gun."

Venison was a staple to many Islanders' diets. Hunting season or not, if meat was needed, a deer was shot. Hunting was not just for sport, it provided many meals for many needy families. Pete Oleson said of Doc's hunting, "I think Doc accepted the premise that game was provided for man by God for his

Doc Farmer Doc Farmer Doc Farmer Doc Farmer Doc Farmer Doc Farmer Doc Farmer Doc Farmer Doc Farmer Doc Farmer Doc Farmer Doc Farmer

103

sustenance. As far as I know, he never killed just for the enjoyment."

"Doc was quite the pirate," laughs Herb Gibson. "He used to take my dad hunting for fresh venison even out of season."

Everett Gunnlaugsson used to hunt with Doc on the Island. "We did a lot of night hunting, and we gave the deer to the poor elderly people. Doc was a dead shot. If he missed the first time, he would be mad at himself."

Jane Farmer Kane said, "Dad carried one shell claiming 'that's all you need'."

Jim Anderson remembers the story about Doc hunting rabbits with Ernie Lockhart. Ernie got between Doc and the rabbit, and Doc accidentally shot him in the rump. Instead of going back to the office, Doc bent Ernie over a log and plucked the buckshot out on the spot.

Everett Gunnlaugsson was with Doc and Ernie hunting rabbits, and said, "We were hunting rabbits out behind Roy Anderson's place and it was thick with cedars and brush. Doc saw a rabbit and shot; Ernie just happened to be in the way. Doc told him to drop his pants, and he pulled out his jack-knife and picked the pieces of shot out. Ernie never uttered a word."

In Norbert Blei's book, *Door Way*, Doc tells about one of his experiences.

Doc Farmer Doc farmer Doc Farmer Doc farmer Doc Farmer Doc farmer Doc Farmer Doc farmer Doc Farmer Doc farmer Doc Farmer Doc farmer

104

"One time I was out tracking deer," he laughs, "and a gal came into the house in labor. Well they sent a guy out to look for me, and I spotted him, but I kept trying to lose him because I thought he was trying to horn in on our deer, heh, heh, heh. But, oh, I got back on time. Everything was all right."

This story actually belongs to Jeanie Hutchens. She told it this way:

"My daughter, Holly, was born December 26, 1952; I went into labor in the morning trimming the Christmas tree. My mother Agnes told me I was in labor and took me to see Doc. His wife Ruby advised us Doc was out hunting. When my water broke, we headed for Pearl's confinement home. Pearl's husband Carl, combed the woods trying to find Doc. Doc arrived about a half hour before Holly was delivered. He got a good chewing out by Ruby, Pearl and Mom. 'Heh, heh, heh, I got here' was all Doc could respond."

Jack Hagen was with Doc hunting this particular time, "Back then there were no "seasons" for deer. We hunted whenever meat was needed," Jack explains. "When Carl came looking for us, we tried to avoid him but he was so persistent, Doc finally decided he had better check to see if he was needed at Pearls."

Bruce Anderson told about the time his father had just started bow hunting. Those were

Doc Farmer Doc farmer Doc Farmer Doc farmer Doc Farmer Doc farmer Doc Farmer Doc farmer Doc Farmer Doc farmer Doc Farmer Doc farmer

105

the times when the arrow didn't have feathers, which meant you had to bend over to get the string onto the nock.

"It was very difficult," Bruce explains, "and Dad walked right into a point."

They pulled the arrow out backwards and called Doc.

"Always one to get a patient's mind off the pain, Doc said, 'Well, at least you drew blood today! And, by the way,' he said to my mother, 'I need a Kotex and a belt.' She said, 'What?' He explained he didn't want to sew the wound closed because infection might set up so he would just put a pad on the area."

'You know you guys would have been better off if you had pulled that arrow all the way through!' Doc added, 'You were about an inch away from the femoral artery.'"

Doc was on call when he was fishing, too. If any of the Islanders needed him the ferry would blow a special signal on the horn for him. Doc's daughter, Jane, said her dad preferred to hunt rather than fish because fishing was too stationary.

Doc was an outdoorsman. He often wore a Sherlock Holmes or modified deerstalker looking hat, wool shirts, and ankle-high lace up boots when making house calls on the spur of the moment.

Doc Farmer Doc farmer Doc Farmer Doc farmer Doc Farmer Doc farmer Doc Farmer Doc farmer Doc Farmer Doc farmer Doc Farmer Doc farmer

106

Hunting, fishing, and doctoring--who has time to change clothes when one is the only doctor and always on call?

Doc making a 'spur of the moment' house call

Doc Farmer Doc farmer Doc Farmer Doc farmer Doc Farmer Doc farmer Doc Farmer Doc farmer Doc Farmer Doc farmer Doc Farmer Doc farmer

107

"Quick, man, quick! It's a matter life or death—a hundred chances on death to one on life, I'll never forgive myself never, if we are too late!"

--Sherlock Holmes in 'The Disappearance of Lady Frances Carfax'

Ebb and Flow of Life

Doc and death were on a first name basis. Although he fought death's appearance, with every tool in his worn black bag, he was a realist. He learned early to detect death's cold expiration breathing down his neck. As Pete Oleson said:

"Doc had an uncanny accuracy for predicting death. If he said, 'She's got about 3 weeks'—it was usually 19 to 22 days. I never knew him to be wrong. Glad I wasn't one of his statistics."

Statistics didn't interest Doc; what interested him were people and their health. Empathetic to the last, Doc was often an interrupter of death's mission, but when it was time to refer to a Higher Authority, Doc relinquished control.

When Doc's brother, Bob, came to visit the family on the Island, Doc told him he didn't have long to live. As it turned out, he only lived to be 58.

Doc Farmer Doc farmer Doc Farmer Doc farmer Doc Farmer Doc farmer Doc Farmer Doc farmer Doc Farmer Doc farmer Doc Farmer Doc farmer

108

When Barbara and Ray Hansen's first baby died, Barbara says she needed Doc's calming words and understanding heart as she explains:

"I don't think Doc had psychiatric training but he knew what to say. When my first baby Paula died of what they now call sudden infant death syndrome or crib death at eighteen months, we called Doc. He was there in five minutes. I was already pregnant with my second child (Doug) and I was hysterical.

"Doc, I know you can save her!" Barbara said she pleaded. "She had already died before Doc had gotten there but I was sure he could do something."

Doc said, 'I'm sorry, Barbara, I am not God.'

"I went in the corner and turned my back on Ray and Doc," Barbara continues. "I felt like I was going to lose it. Doc walked over, put his hand on my pregnant stomach and said, 'I believe the baby has dropped, it won't be long.' It brought me back, to know that I couldn't go there. He was a very wise man."

Death linked Doc and Clyde Casperson (Casperson's Funeral Home, Sister Bay) together, as Clyde recounts;

"The first I remember meeting Doc was on Washington Island. I, as a Funeral Director would have to go to him to have a death certificate signed when one of his patients died.

Doc Farmer Doc farmer Doc Farmer Doc farmer Doc Farmer Doc farmer Doc Farmer Doc farmer Doc Farmer Doc farmer Doc Farmer Doc farmer

109

Many a night, I would have to stay on the Island and we would wind up having dinner together.

When he moved to Sister Bay, the clinic was our neighbor. Doc Farmer and Dr. March became our family doctors and remained so until their retirements.

What I remember most of Doc Farmer was his love and concern for all of his patients. It was of no concern of his if they were poor, rich or what area they came from. He gave his all, his best professional treatment.

If there was a death, no matter what hour of the day or night, he would stay with the family until the funeral director arrived.

Clyde and Mila Casperson

I could fill many pages with stories of the experiences in practice this good doctor had.

Doc Farmer Doc farmer Doc Farmer Doc farmer Doc Farmer Doc farmer Doc Farmer Doc farmer Doc Farmer Doc farmer Doc Farmer Doc farmer

110

Better his memory will always be with us. God bless Doc, we miss you."

No matter what hour of the day or night was certainly the truth. Mildred Goodman Jacobsen recalls the night her sister-in-law, Alma Jessen, died at age forty-seven. Alma had an especially debilitating case of diabetes and asthma. Both had taken a toll on her body. When Doc was called, he didn't take time to dress; he rushed down in his pajamas. Alma had already had a heart attack, and there wasn't anything Doc could do to save her; but his vigil didn't end there, as Mildred explains:

"Alma was my husband Paul's sister and she had come to visit us that day. Paul had picked some apples for her, and he had to climb the tree to get them. Back then applesauce and honey was believed to help asthma sufferers."

'You didn't have to do that!' Alma said.

'Oh yes I did,' Paul told her.

Both Mildred and Paul had a hard time getting to sleep that night so when the knock came at their door, they both were apprehensive about opening it. There stood Don (Alma's son) and Doc. 'Don't be frightened,' Doc told them. That's when they learned of Alma's death.

"Doc was always there for you," Mildred said, "even if it meant coming on the spur of the moment in his pajamas."

Doc Farmer Doc farmer Doc Farmer Doc farmer Doc Farmer Doc farmer Doc Farmer Doc farmer Doc Farmer Doc farmer Doc Farmer Doc farmer

111

Pain comes in all guises as Jane Farmer Kane remembers riding with her father on some of his calls.

"A family was having a reunion and a man collapsed and died. They called dad, and it was a twenty minute ride to get there. The folks couldn't believe dad couldn't do anything to save the man. They begged and pleaded, 'Please, Please, do something!.' All dad could say was, "I'm sorry; there is nothing I can do. If you will call Casperson's (funeral home), I'll wait here with you."

Another time Jane recalls a motorcycle accident in Northport, where a woman had died. "They kept asking Dad, 'Are you sure? Are you sure she is dead???'"

Doc tells about one patient with cancer and another who couldn't afford to go to the hospital in an interview with Norbert Blei in the book, *Door Way*:

"I had a patient too who was dying of cancer. Oh, he knew it. There wasn't much we could do. He was all skin and bones. 'I'd jump out the window, Doc,' heh, heh, heh, 'only it's not high enough.' Well you'd like to be able to take them outside and shoot them like a lame horse when it's that bad. I left him some morphine to ease the pain. "Don't take more than half of it, or you'll be dead," I told him. He took it all."

And ... "I was visiting an old couple the other day. He's 89 and she's in her 80's. Neither of them getting any Medicare. They can hardly make taxes. And they can't afford to pay $6.50 a month off their social security for Medicare. The old guy should go to the hospital. But he said to me, 'No, I'll just stay here and die. We need that money to live on.' Most of their diet is potatoes and oatmeal."

It irked Doc that old people who could not even afford protein in their diets should have to pay school taxes.

For Doc, fighting the grim reaper was part of his everyday existence, and he learned and helped others learn to deal with the cold nature of death. The one thing he could not tolerate or understand was the cold nature of bureaucracy. Doc was constantly working for the health and best interests of his patients and it often seemed to Doc that bureaucracy was in the ring with death fighting against his patients and raising the costs of health.

In a 1974 article in the *Door County Advocate*, Keta Steebs says:

For 45 years Dr. E. C. Farmer of Sister Bay has been battling the elements, the Grim Reaper and government agencies. His box score with the weather has been pretty good, he's won his share of victories over death but when it comes to tilting bureaucratic

Doc Farmer Doc farmer Doc Farmer Doc farmer Doc Farmer Doc farmer Doc Farmer Doc farmer Doc Farmer Doc farmer Doc Farmer Doc farmer

113

windmills the good doctor's win column stays close to zilch.

She goes on to say that battling the elements and Grim Reaper pale in comparison to the *"almost daily skirmishes Farmer engages in with the powers that be in Madison."*

"One faceless foe, either a secretary or file clerk, he (Doc) isn't sure which, particularly irritates him. She can't understand why a doctor would be making house calls in this day and age and is, says Farmer, 'pretty snippy about the whole thing.' "If people are sick enough for a doctor," she told him recently, "they belong in a hospital. Medicare pays for hospitalization; it does not pay for house calls."

"I've had to quit calling on Medicare patients just because of that stupid ruling," he says with more than a hint of bitterness in his voice. "What's so ironic is that I could have kept this one elderly couple out of an institution and in their own home, which is where they want to be, for less than a day's hospital care costs."

Keta continues in the article,

"Because Medicare won't pay his $5 fee (plus mileage one way) Farmer said this once self-reliant pair is now costing the government something like

$1000 a month. The man is suffering from rheumatoid arthritis, which confines him to a wheelchair, and his wife is anemic but they were able to manage quite well with once a month shots of cortisone, in his case and B-12 vitamins in hers. Now they are in a nursing home and 'cry a lot.'"

In the article Doc talks about another 48 year old woman suffering from malignant hypertension who had been 'futilely applying for disability benefits.'

"They turned her down flat every time, ...she died working at a job she was in no condition to be doing...They told her, "You're still working aren't you? If you can work you don't need social security."

Doc told Keta about a patient *'who had suffered from recurring dizzy spells from a brain condition which refused to respond to treatment. He had to quit his job at a local shipyard because he could no longer climb.' When Doc referred him to the social security administration, they sent him to a Green Bay specialist who told the man,*

"So, you get dizzy; so you're afraid you're going to fall and kill yourself, so that's a chance we all take. I might get killed in my car on the way home tonight."

Doc Farmer Doc farmer Doc Farmer Doc farmer Doc Farmer Doc farmer Doc Farmer Doc farmer Doc Farmer Doc farmer Doc Farmer Doc farmer

115

For a woman suffering from epilepsy, Madison recommended she attend vocational training or take a job babysitting. Doc said, "Who in the devil would be around to take care of the baby if she suffered an epileptic seizure?...I don't know how many phone calls I've made or how much hell I've raised with those boneheads down there but it looks like she's finally going to get the benefits she's entitled too."

Doc goes on spouting to Keta:

"You'd think the damn money was coming out of their pocket. ...They sure hate to certify a person as being eligible even when some of them are half dead."

You have to love the man. Who would not want Doc on his side and in his ring fighting the weather, the bureaucracy or the Grim Reaper?

Doc Farmer Doc farmer Doc Farmer Doc farmer Doc Farmer Doc farmer Doc Farmer Doc farmer Doc Farmer Doc farmer Doc Farmer Doc farmer

116

"To let the brain work without sufficient material is like racing an engine. It racks itself to pieces."
–Sherlock Holmes in 'The Adventures of the Devil's Foot'

More than Just a Sum of Body Parts

Body manipulations and bone repositioning were Doc's specialty as an Osteopath.

In Norbert Blei's book, *Door Way*, Doc says of Osteopathy:

"A. T. Still began it. He was known as the bone doctor. His idea was that the rule of the artery was supreme. You free up the circulation, and you get health."

Everyone who ever had their back or neck adjusted by Doc long for the pleasure of Doc's hands. Dr. Jack March who worked with Doc agrees, "Doc Farmer was an Osteopathic doctor. He had the ability to work with his hands. If any of my patients came to see me with whiplash," Dr. March explains, "I would send them to Doc. If they got to him within 24-48 hours, they got over the whiplash; if they waited too long, the whiplash would set. He knew what he was doing."

Doc Farmer Doc Farmer Doc Farmer Doc Farmer Doc Farmer Doc Farmer Doc Farmer Doc Farmer Doc Farmer Doc Farmer Doc Farmer

117

Andrea Lundquist, who also worked with Doc at the Sister Bay Clinic, said, "It would amaze me how Doc would come up behind you, the patient, and tell you to relax; he would then adjust your back into realignment."

Hannes Andersen said, "Glennie was riding with George Hanson, and they hit a culvert. Glennie hit the windshield. His teeth hit the rounded dash, and he ended up with a badly broken jaw. Doc Farmer set it for him and flew him away to Sturgeon Bay. Dr. Dorchester x-rayed the jaw; it was set perfectly. Dr. Dorchester said to Glennie, "If ever I have a broken bone, there is only one doctor who will set it; Farmer is the man for me"

Jeanie Hutchens agreed; "I remember one time having a stiff neck, I was walking through the door, and Doc grabbed me and straightened me right out."

It seems the element of surprise was what Doc liked. The adjustments seemed to work better when people were relaxed. If his patients were unaware that Doc was going to adjust their neck or back or whatever, the less likely they were to tense up.

His hands on approach gave Doc an edge when it came to diagnosing illness. Doc took the Osteopathic Oath to heart.

Doc Farmer Doc farmer Doc Farmer Doc farmer Doc Farmer Doc farmer Doc Farmer Doc farmer Doc Farmer Doc farmer Doc Farmer Doc farmer

118

The Osteopathic Oath

I do hereby affirm my loyalty to the profession I am about to enter. I will be mindful always of my great responsibility to preserve the health and the life of my patients, to retain their confidence and respect both as a physician and a friend who will guard their secrets with scrupulous honor and fidelity, to perform faithfully my professional duties, to employ only those recognized methods of treatment consistent with good judgment and with my skill and ability, keeping in mind always nature's laws and the body's inherent capacity for recovery.

I will be ever vigilant in aiding in the general welfare of the community, sustaining its laws and institutions, not engaging in those practices which will in any way bring shame or discredit upon myself or my profession. I will give no drugs for deadly purposes to any person, though it may be asked of me. I will endeavor to work in accord with my colleagues in a spirit of progressive cooperation and never by word or by act cast imputations upon them or their rightful practices.

I will look with respect and esteem upon all those who have taught me my art. To my college I will be loyal and strive always for its best interests and for the interests of the students who will come after me. I will be ever alert to further the application of basic biologic truths to the healing arts and to develop the principles of osteopathy which were first enunciated by Andrew Taylor Still.

Doc Farmer Doc farmer Doc Farmer Doc farmer Doc Farmer Doc farmer Doc Farmer Doc farmer Doc Farmer Doc farmer Doc Farmer Doc farmer

119

The American Osteopathic Association says of Osteopathy:

"You are more than just the sum of your body parts. That's why doctors of osteopathic medicine (D.O.s) practice a "whole person" approach to health care. Instead of just treating specific symptoms, osteopathic physicians concentrate on treating you as a whole.

Osteopathic physicians understand how all the body's systems are interconnected and how each one affects the others. They focus special attention on the musculoskeletal system, which reflects and influences the condition of all other body systems.

This system of bones and muscles makes up about two thirds of the body's mass, and a routine part of the examination D.O.s give patients is a careful evaluation of these important structures. D.O.s know that the body's structure plays a critical role in its ability to function. They can use their eyes and hands to identify structural problems and to support the body's natural tendency toward health and self-healing.

Osteopathic physicians also use their ears to listen to you and your health concerns. D.O.s help patients develop attitudes and lifestyles that don't just fight illness but also help prevent it. Millions of

Doc Farmer Doc farmer Doc Farmer Doc farmer Doc Farmer Doc farmer Doc Farmer Doc farmer Doc Farmer Doc farmer Doc Farmer Doc farmer

120

Americans prefer this concerned and compassionate care and have made D.O.s their physicians for life"

Oh to have Doc Farmer as our physician for life! We surely miss you Doc and your hands-on, compassionate, empathetic know-how.

Anyway, the world can not go back to the Doc Farmer days of unmitigated care, but we can use what he taught us about true doctoring to find the right doctor at the right time.

The right doctor at the right time is what the John O'Briens of Chicago found in Sister Bay when they needed plasma for their ten-year-old son Dan. In July 1963, the O'Briens arrived in Fish Creek on their cabin cruiser. They were hoping Dan could have a calming vacation before returning to a Chicago hospital for treatment for the rest of the summer. Dan had hemophilia and the internal bleeding had done damage to his knees and elbows. But the calm vacation was not to be as Dan started suffering intense pain from the disease. The O'Briens always carried two units of the plasma with them, but these two units were not enough to stop the pain. They sought the help of Dr. Farmer. An article in *the Door County Advocate* July 9, 1963 states:

"After making numerous phone calls, Dr. Farmer located one unit of the plasma at Madison and

Doc Farmer Doc farmer Doc Farmer Doc farmer Doc Farmer Doc farmer Doc Farmer Doc farmer Doc Farmer Doc farmer Doc Farmer Doc farmer

121

it was rushed to Door County. Finally, through Chicago Blood Donor Services, Dr. Farmer located an additional supply of the plasma. Two units were rushed to Door County Wednesday and three more on Friday.... As soon as the plasma arrived at Dr. Farmer's office, it was thawed and readied for use. The plasma must be used within three hours after it is thawed."

The article goes on to say :

... "Dr. Farmer, who obtained the necessary plasma administered the transfusions, explained that in a hemophilia victim minor bleeding from external cuts and scratches is not a serious problem because it can be controlled by pressure, but that internal bleeding is extremely serious because it cannot be halted in this manner. Even the extraction of a tooth is a grave matter, he said, because of inability to stop resultant bleeding.

Both Mr. and Mrs. O'Brien expressed deep gratitude for efforts that were made on behalf of their son. O'Brien, who is an optometrist in Chicago, was profuse in his praise."

Doc's knowledge of the 'whole body' helped him through many emergency situations. Lorna Bell Cornell feels Doc saved her life in one such emergency:

"It was the summer of 1950 on Washington Island. I was about nine or ten

Doc Farmer Doc farmer Doc Farmer Doc farmer Doc Farmer Doc farmer Doc Farmer Doc farmer Doc Farmer Doc farmer Doc Farmer Doc farmer

122

years old and I was leaving a movie at Nelson's Hall. Those were the times the roads were gravel. One of the teenagers pulled out of the parking area spinning his wheels. He stirred up so much dust I went into a full-blown asthma attack. It was really scary because there were no ferry boats running and flying off the Island was an impossibility. Doc Farmer was our only hope so Dad took me to him. Doc gave, what looked to me like, a horse pill and told my dad,

'Bob, If you can get her to settle down and be real quiet, this might work, but if it doesn't, bring her back for a tracheotomy.'

We went home and dad set up some lawn chairs outside. He got a bunch of army blankets to keep us warm and we sat and talked about the stars half the night. The problem broke. In a sense, Doc saved my life."

Asthma was a problem for Matthew Goodman too. His mother, Mildred Goodman Jacobsen explains, "Matt had asthma real bad. When he was given a certain medicine, he had to be watched day and night. His dad Paul, whose job was commercial fishing, was fishing from sunup to sundown. Ruby would come spell me during the afternoon and Doc watched Matt at night so Paul could get some sleep. Another time, daughter Ruth was screaming in pain from an attack of appendicitis and Paul couldn't be reached on the lake so Doc drove with us to the Sturgeon Bay Hospital".

Doc Farmer Doc farmer Doc Farmer Doc farmer Doc Farmer Doc farmer Doc Farmer Doc farmer Doc Farmer Doc farmer Doc Farmer Doc farmer

123

If Doc and Ruby had charged the going rate for the one-on-one personal care they provided, all of us patients would still be paying on the indebtedness. Not only the bodily healing but psychological mending came in the door with Doc.

Doc treated everyone as 'more than just a sum of the parts', as Wally Mickelson penned:

> *In the village of Sister Bay*
> *Just before the road bends*
> *You will find in the Nor-Dor clinic*
> *A man with a million friends*
> *His kindness and humility*
> *Came from hardy stock*
> *To all of us who know him*
> *He is our well-loved "Good Old Doc."*

Doc Farmer Doc farmer Doc Farmer Doc farmer Doc Farmer Doc farmer Doc Farmer Doc farmer Doc Farmer Doc farmer Doc Farmer Doc farmer

124

"Our highest assurance of the goodness of Providence seems to me to rest in the flowers. All other things, our powers, our desires, our food, are all really necessary for our existence in the first instance. But this rose is an extra. Its smell and its colour are an embellishment of life, not a condition of it. It is only goodness which gives extras and so I say again that we have much to hope from the flowers."

–Sherlock Holmes in 'The Naval Treaty'

Hope From the Flowers

Doc's sanity saver was his garden. He would putter in his garden any spare moment he had. If he showed up with dirt under his fingernails, it was only because he left his garden STAT when called. His daughter, Jane, said he put soap under his fingernails to try to keep as much dirt out as possible but anyone who gardens knows that to grow flowers and vegetables, one needs to dig in the dirt.

"Dad loved gardening," Jane laughs. "One day I came upon him hoeing and mumbling under his breath, 'I make life and death decisions everyday....' It was very good therapy,"

Jane added. "The garden on the Island had rows and rows of vegetables and flower beds full of roses. A few fruit trees too. Mom canned and pickled jars of fruit, filling up shelves in the basement. One of my favorites was pickled crab apples with sugar and cinnamon!"

Doc Farmer Doc farmer Doc Farmer Doc farmer Doc Farmer Doc farmer Doc Farmer Doc farmer Doc Farmer Doc farmer Doc Farmer Doc farmer

125

Joy Gunnlaugsson remembers Doc's failed attempt to grow blueberries. He even stuck nails in the ground to invigorate the soil, with no luck. He was constantly trying new varieties of seeds.

"Doc was an organic farmer. He had a big, big garden in the back and to the left of his house. He grew the most phenomenal produce," Carol Richter Lemon said. "We used to sneak in to eat his carrots. He was ahead of his time."

Doc believed in the natural. He tried to eat healthy and tried to convince anyone who would listen as he states in Norbert Blei's book, *Door Way*:

"In the early days, growing up on the farm, we didn't use any poisons. There are over 3,000 additives in foods today that nobody's ever even examined. We don't know what the hell they could be doing to us. You know a mouse or a rat will never eat baker's white bread.

We need protein every day. It should be mostly farm raised soybeans, cheese, yogurt...lots of salads, fruits, vegetables. I've got peaches, plums and walnuts here. None of them sprayed. Unpasteurized milk, if you like it, but you don't need it. And supplement this all with natural vitamins and minerals. No white flour, no white sugar. Use honey.

Doc Farmer Doc farmer Doc Farmer Doc farmer Doc Farmer Doc farmer Doc Farmer Doc farmer Doc Farmer Doc farmer Doc Farmer Doc farmer

126

...Vitamin E, good for circulatory problems. I take 1600 milligrams each day. I take a multiple vitamin that has everything in it. I take 5000 milligrams of vitamin C each day; 20,000 milligrams of vitamin A; four A&D capsules, that's cod liver oil. I take four manganese pills, two lecithin capsules, two vitamin B complex, two desiccated liver pills a day, four bone meal tablets; brewers yeast on my cereal; one kelp tablet a day; one zinc tablet; vitamin B6, four a day; and two tablespoons of bran. I have two eggs for breakfast, but never hard boiled or fried. Only poached or soft boiled to keep the lecithin."

Connie Scmitt Essig said Doc always told her if you take antibiotics, drink buttermilk or eat yogurt because it has acidophilus to restore the good bacteria in your system. Doc practiced probiotics ('for life') concepts before much was known about the ill effects of antibiotics. Probiotics support the immune system and Doc was a big advocate of the 'whole health of every individual.'

At his home in Sister Bay, he had a beautiful flower garden. Andrea Lundquist (Doc's medical assistant in Sister Bay) said Doc was known for his roses. Every Monday he would bring a new rose into the office and every Friday she got to take it home. Everyone knew Doc's roses. Doc was a nurturer. "It comes from inside," Andrea says, "Doc loved nurturing that is why he had such a great garden."

"In Sister Bay our home had about four acres of lawn, trees and gardens," Jane remembers. "In these modern times, fruits and vegetables are frozen for winter enjoyment, but back then there was a root cellar in the back yard where bushels of apples and potatoes were stored."

Farmer home in Sister Bay

Doc Farmer Doc farmer Doc Farmer Doc farmer Doc Farmer Doc farmer Doc Farmer Doc farmer Doc Farmer Doc farmer Doc Farmer Doc farmer

128

Dr. March said, "Doc planted trees to yield fruit, had a huge garden out behind the house, and cut his own grass. He also loved birds and had several birdfeeders."

There is a correlation between a good doctor and a good gardener: each strives for healthy robust species; each diagnoses and fights disease, insects, and parasites; each searches out the right nutrients; each lovingly, empathetically, and caringly tends the tender shoots. Each hoes out the strangling weeds and encourages growth. Each knows from whence the water, sunshine, and beauty come.

Doc was both a good doctor and a good gardener. He was always striving to understand the health of plants and by so doing hoping to understand the health of men, as Lord Alfred Tennyson so succinctly wrote:

> *Flower in the crannied wall,*
> *I pluck you out of the crannies,*
> *I hold you here, root and all, in my hand,*
> *Little flower -but if I could understand*
> *What you are, root and all, and all in all,*
> *I should know what God and man is.*

Doc Farmer Doc farmer Doc Farmer Doc farmer Doc Farmer Doc farmer Doc Farmer Doc farmer Doc Farmer Doc farmer Doc Farmer Doc farmer

129

"I am an omnivorous reader with a strangely retentive memory for trifles."

--Sherlock Holmes in 'The Adeventure of the Lion's Mane'

On Their Side

Doc had several hobbies. Besides gardening, he collected coins, enjoyed woodworking and even dabbled in poetry. When he was courting Ruby, he wrote these two ditties:

Since you've gone away from me my sweet
I'm lonesome, sad and blue
The reason dear is plain to see
I miss a "MISS" it's you.

I miss the sweetness of your smile
Your hands to hold and kiss
I'd really like to let you know
It's you "SWEET GIRL" I miss.

On every nite when you're away
I miss you so, and thru the day
You fill my every waking hour,
With thoughts of you, and say----

Doc Farmer Doc farmer Doc Farmer Doc farmer Doc Farmer Doc farmer Doc Farmer Doc farmer Doc Farmer Doc farmer Doc Farmer Doc farmer

130

I need you dear and can't you see
Where'ere you are, your part of me
I need the loveliness of you
Because my dear I love but thee.

E. C. Farmer 11/25/38

TO A SWEET GIRL FROM A LONESOME LAD

To you my dear I write this note
    And mail to you today,
To tell you how sweet you are
    My precious; Adorable and say---
Have I told you how I love you
    And worship you my dear?
All life to me is emptiness
    Unless you my sweet, are near.
I love the beauty of your smile
    Your lips of ruby hue,
 Your hair, your eyes, your skin so soft
    That are--the loveliness of you.
So I'll give this to Uncle Sam
    To deliver--and convey to you
All my love for all my life,
    Darling; I'll always be true.

E. C. Farmer

One of Doc's favorite pastimes was reading. Spare time was at a premium, so he

Doc Farmer Doc farmer Doc Farmer Doc farmer Doc Farmer Doc farmer Doc Farmer Doc farmer Doc Farmer Doc farmer Doc Farmer Doc farmer

131

selected his reading materials with care. According to his daughter, Jane, "After going to college in Chicago, Dad subscribed to the *Chicago Tribune*. He read it his whole life. He read medical journals, *Argosy Magazine*, *Popular Mechanics*, hunting and outdoor magazines, and mysteries. There was an author of police mysteries, *57th Precinct* that the whole family enjoyed."

Mysteries being one of Doc's favorite genres of fiction, I can't help but think he read every Sherlock Holmes mystery Sir Arthur Conan Doyle ever wrote. And since Doc was proud of his English ancestry, he also must have been intrigued by the scenery around London so well described in Sherlock's wanderings.

This intrigue led to a longing to travel. Doc didn't get to travel much until after his marriage to Margaret (after Ruby died in 1967) and his semi-retirement. Doc never actually retired. He still saw patients one day a week at his home up until his second stroke in 1979. He and Margaret traveled to Australia, Alaska and England. Dr. March and his wife Margaret traveled with Doc and Margaret around Lake Superior for one vacation.

The trip to Alaska was given as a gift to Doc and Margaret at "Doc Farmer Day" by the people of Northern Door County. In a *Door County Advocate* article written by Keta Steebs, she said,

Doc Farmer Doc farmer Doc Farmer Doc farmer Doc Farmer Doc farmer Doc Farmer Doc farmer Doc Farmer Doc farmer Doc Farmer Doc farmer

132

"...*Sunday June 22, (1975) was just a day set aside by old friends to honor a country doctor who has never let them down.*" ...*[it] was time, the people decided, to reward such untiring devotion.*" *About 500 people attended the party to thank Doc and to show him how much he meant to them.*"

Norbert Blei had written an article for the "Insight Magazine" in the *Milwaukee Journal* called 'Doc Farmer: That Special Touch.' It was published, June 1, 1975, just twenty-one days before the party. It highly praised Doc and his services to the Door. The *Journal* article ended with,

"*So it must be this common sense style of doctoring that the people take a liking to. A doctor who never charges them much, fixes them up just fine to keep going till the next time, and, most significantly, seems to be on their side. If you can't trust the politicians these days, at least you can trust Doc Farmer.*"

According to Keta's *Advocate* article: "*So, long time friend and master of ceremonies at Doc Farmer Day, Pete Oleson, had to poke fun at Doc by saying that after this article,*

"*Doc now sits at Al's Restaurant the better part of each morning signing autographs and charges people to hear the punch line to his innumerable jokes*

Doc Farmer Doc farmer Doc Farmer Doc farmer Doc Farmer Doc farmer Doc Farmer Doc farmer Doc Farmer Doc farmer Doc Farmer Doc farmer

133

but other than that 'this humble man remains the same'."

Remaining the same was what Doc did. He was always a man to trust to be there when called, to never let us down and his calling as a doctor opened the Door to healing.

Milwaukee Journal, dated 1 June 1975, R. Brodzeller photographer, © 2007 Journal Sentinel Inc., reproduced with permission

Doc Farmer Doc farmer Doc Farmer Doc farmer Doc Farmer Doc farmer Doc Farmer Doc farmer Doc Farmer Doc farmer Doc Farmer Doc farmer

134

"Education, Gregson, education. Still seeking knowledge at the old university.

-Sherlock Holmes in 'The Adventure of the Red Circle'

There For You

In Dr. Rachel Naomi Remen's book, *Kitchen Table Wisdom*, she states,

"Everybody is a story. When I was a child, people sat around kitchen tables and told their stories. We don't do that much anymore. Sitting around the table telling stories is not just a way of passing time. It is the way the wisdom gets passed along. The stuff that helps us to live a life worth remembering. ...The stories we can tell each other have no beginning and ending. They are a front-row seat to the real experience.

...The kitchen table is a level playing field. Everyone's story matters. ...Stories that touch us in this place of common humanness awaken us and weave us together as a family once again."

For Doc, sitting at the kitchen table while eating homemade pie, cake or cookies with a cup of coffee, tea or 'hot sling' was the time for stories—listening and telling. Whenever he made house calls, if he did not have pressing issues, he would take the time to sit at the

Doc Farmer Doc Farmer Doc Farmer Doc Farmer Doc Farmer Doc Farmer Doc Farmer Doc Farmer Doc Farmer Doc Farmer Doc Farmer Doc Farmer

135

kitchen table and witness the *'front row seat to the real experience.'*

Daughter Jane Farmer Kane recalls many times riding along with her dad on house visits.

"When school was not in session, summer months, and weekends, Dad would invite me to ride along as he made house calls. We enjoyed each others' company! When we arrived at a residence, I usually stayed in the car and patiently waited, or if it was a place on the water, I would wander to the shoreline, and occasionally I would go into the house with Dad—more often when it was a shut-in and Dad was on a routine check of a patient.

There was an elderly couple, Waldemer and Nora Hansen on the Island. I remember Mrs. Hansen as always being in bed, in a room off the kitchen. Dad would have me go into the Hansen's home with him and after checking Mrs. Hansen and her medication supplies, Dad would accept Waldemer's invite to sit and have a 'hot-sling.' The teakettle would already be on the woodstove steaming. He would take two thick mugs, put a spoon of sugar in each, then a shot of whiskey in each, and last fill with boiling water. Sitting at the kitchen table, Mr. Hansen would always have a Kit Kat candy bar for me, as the two men visited a bit.

Sometimes I think that some of Dad's best medicine or medical therapy was sitting at

Doc Farmer Doc farmer Doc Farmer Doc farmer Doc Farmer Doc farmer Doc Farmer Doc farmer Doc Farmer Doc farmer Doc Farmer Doc farmer

136

kitchen tables having coffee and talking with patients and family members."

Waldemer and Nora were Shirley Atkins Ellefson's grandparents. She said that her grandmother had rheumatoid arthritis and Doc would give her daily shots for pain.

"Doc was so good to them," Shirley said "He was very prompt, always good natured and he would give advice over the phone," like the time her son Bruce started drinking at an early age.

Bruce was twenty-three months old when he crawled out of his crib, climbed up to the second shelf in the pantry, and drank three quarters of a bottle of vanilla.

Shirley said, "One doesn't have to be bright to know what happened. I called Doc and he said, 'Well, he's drunk, he'll be ok." Bruce laughed, hiccoughed, talked a blue streak; the 'jag' lasted about 3 to 4 hours. But, he was ok."

Doc would stop in at the store for some groceries and people would ask him to diagnose their child's problem. On the spot, he would examine an ear, or eye, or whatever was ailing the child, and tell the parent what to do.

Doc knew when medicine was needed. If a patient thought they were not getting enough medicine, but Doc thought they did not need medication, he had a little trick. He found an aspirin manufacturer who produced aspirin

Doc Farmer Doc Farmer Doc Farmer Doc Farmer Doc Farmer Doc Farmer Doc Farmer Doc Farmer Doc Farmer Doc Farmer Doc Farmer

137

which was green in color and triangular shaped. He would give these patients this pill and say, 'see how you feel.' Like a placebo, it worked just fine.

"Dad was a minimalist," Jane explains. "He thought less was more, when it came to medicine."

One person who did not take her medicine like she was supposed to was Carol Goodlet O'Neill. "This was around the time everyone was so worried about polio so every summer, when I was up on the Island, Doc would give me penicillin gum," Carol relates. "It had the most disgusting taste, so I spit it out when I got home, and the chickens ate it. Our chickens never had to worry about getting polio. Carol also remembers the many times she visited Doc to get cortisone shots.

"We lived in Jackson Harbor, the poison ivy capital of the Island. One year in particular, I remember having a severe case of poison ivy because I had fallen in it. Doc fixed me up with a cortisone shot, but it took a while for it to go away."

Rip Koken remembers getting poison ivy so bad it was in his eyes.

"Every summer, without fail, my sister Kris and I would get poison ivy. I remember Doc coming into the house with that heh, heh, heh laugh, pipe hanging out of his mouth, and fixing us up the best he could."

Doc Farmer Doc Farmer Doc Farmer Doc Farmer Doc Farmer Doc Farmer Doc Farmer Doc Farmer Doc Farmer Doc Farmer Doc Farmer Doc Farmer

138

Elaine Daubner Mickleson had a scary incident when celebrating her birthday:

"It was my twenty-ninth birthday," Elaine relates, " and with my husband and four children had all my relatives to my house to help celebrate.

The table was set and I was preparing to put the food on, when suddenly, I couldn't breathe. Dr. Farmer was called immediately. He arrived within a short time. He looked at me and said, 'You look like a fugitive from Caspersons' (funeral home).

With his help I could breathe, but in short gasps. He then called Dr. March from the hospital in Algoma, and I was taken to the hospital.

Dr. March said I was too young to have an experience like that. After I was examined and x-rayed, it was found that I had a blood clot in my lung which had passed through.

Dr. Farmer was an invaluable person in our community. He was a perfect family doctor, always there when he was needed.

He had compassion and kindness toward older people, and told jokes to ease their anxiety. He was trusted by all."

Doc was also there for Anita Beckstrom. She said, "We phoned Doc at 3:00 a.m. because my husband had terrible pain in his stomach area. Dr. Farmer made a house call to our home, about a mile away from his home. It was determined that it was gall bladder trouble. We didn't have hospital insurance in those days, and so Doc called and made all the arrangements for treatment at the Veterans Hospital in Milwaukee, as my husband was a veteran. Everything turned out fine.

We will never forget his really off-beat jokes and his wicked chuckle when he told them. He did get his patients to relax a bit. It sure was comforting to know he was there in emergencies. Doc Farmer, the druggist, and the funeral director always met for morning coffee breaks at Al Johnson's Restaurant. We hoped that they weren't really in cahoots!"

Jane Farmer Kane remembers her dad "being there" for a migrant worker who was badly burned.

"The workers were sitting around a camp fire," Jane explained, "when one of the children tripped. Before he could fall into the fire, the child's dad caught him but the dad fell in the fire. His back was badly burned and dad put A&D ointment on him, bandaged him and told him to only wear cotton shirts. The man came back every day, but he never complained because he had saved his child's life."

People did not know but Doc kept an eye out for signs of domestic violence. He was close friends with Sheriff Baldy Bridenhagen and worked with 'Baldy' reporting any physical abuse he found.

Doc Farmer Doc farmer Doc Farmer Doc farmer Doc Farmer Doc farmer Doc Farmer Doc farmer Doc Farmer Doc farmer Doc Farmer Doc farmer

140

Keeping an open eye and ear was Doc's way of being there and aware.

Dr. Remen in her book, *Kitchen Table Wisdom*, states it this way:

"Whatever the expertise we have acquired, the greatest gift we bring to anyone who is suffering is our wholeness. Listening is the oldest and perhaps the most powerful tool of healing. It is often through the quality of our listening and not the wisdom of our words that we are able to effect the most profound changes in the people around us. ...Our listening creates sanctuary for the homeless parts within the other person. That which has been denied, unloved, devalued by themselves and by others. That which is hidden. ...Listening creates a holy silence.

Eventually you may be able to hear, in everyone and beyond everyone, the unseen singing softly to itself and to you."

And, *"wounded people can best be healed by other wounded people. Only other wounded people can understand what is needed, for the healing of suffering is compassion not expertise."*

Doc Farmer Doc farmer Doc Farmer Doc farmer Doc Farmer Doc farmer Doc Farmer Doc farmer Doc Farmer Doc farmer Doc Farmer Doc farmer

141

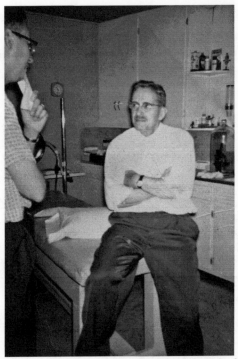

Doc listening, 'perhaps the most powerful tool of healing'

The medical vernacular for compassion, empathy, listening, and attitude is bedside manner. Doc had a great bedside manner— rough as a cob on the outside but oh so tender on the inside with an 'ear' for listening and a heart for being there.

Florence Jess in a Door County Advocate Article dated October 28, 1954, describes Doc's tender side this way:

Doc Farmer Doc farmer Doc Farmer Doc farmer Doc Farmer Doc farmer Doc Farmer Doc farmer Doc Farmer Doc farmer Doc Farmer Doc farmer

142

Here on Washington Island we believe we have the finest medical care of any rural community in the county. Our Dr. E. Farmer has about 750 patients during the winter months and many tourists during the summer season. He has a guaranteed income which we all are glad to contribute to. We have no hospital here so in cases that require hospitalization or severe accidents, he calls a plane from Sturgeon Bay and the patients are flown out to the hospital. In case this should happen during the night, plenty of cars volunteer to light up the airport landing strip. He is assisted by his very capable wife, a graduate nurse, whose skill and engaging bedside manner has made her as one patient put it, "well worth while to the sick" to have her wait on him.

They have two girls, Sara and Jane. In addition to all his patients, he finds time to care for a splendidly kept garden and he modestly will show a caller a wall full of blue ribbons he has received from his flowers. He also finds time to gather mushrooms, of which he is very fond.

The doctor is strictly the home loving type. As an example, your reporter refers to an old lady patient who was not responsive to his treatments. After studying her he thought he detected a disturbed look in her eyes. He saw a sink full of dirty dishes, heated some water, washed the dishes and swept the floor and

Doc Farmer Doc farmer Doc Farmer Doc farmer Doc Farmer Doc farmer Doc Farmer Doc farmer Doc Farmer Doc farmer Doc Farmer Doc farmer

143

by that time the patient was relaxed and sleeping soundly.

Dr. Farmer is also one of our most active civic workers and is on the board of directors of many of our business places. Your reporter would like to take this opportunity to thank for everyone Dr. Farmer and his wife for the care they are giving us.

Ruby and Doc Farmer 1963
(Photo Courtesy Hagedorn Studio)

Doc Farmer Doc farmer Doc Farmer Doc farmer Doc Farmer Doc farmer Doc Farmer Doc farmer Doc Farmer Doc farmer Doc Farmer Doc farmer

144

"We must strike while the iron is hot."
--Sherlock Holmes in 'The Adventure of the Cardboard Box'

Move To Sister Bay

June 1, 1957, Doc and his family--Ruby, Sara, and Jane, moved to Sister Bay. The decision to leave the Island was prompted by several key issues. Doc said it was because his girls wanted to pursue music and would have more opportunities 'down the County,' and the population of the Island was decreasing.

But there were underlying reasons also. When Doc dabbled in politics as Island chairman in 1955-1956, he became disenchanted with the powers of control.

Joy Gunnlaugsson said, "One of the things Doc did in office as Town Chairman was to get a road built to the east side of the Island. Many called it "Farmer's Folly" because a lot of Islanders thought it was a waste of Island funds. The detractors said he had that road put in just so he could hunt on the east side."

This left a bad taste in Doc's mouth. Along with this, Ruby's health was deteriorating. A friend of Doc's, Sam Subin, was instrumental in talking Doc into moving to Sister Bay.

According to an article in the *Door County Advocate* dated April 12, 1973:

"Nor-Dor Medical Center was organized in April, 1957 and for a time occupied space in a Sister Bay residential building. Dr. E. C. Farmer at that time moved from Washington Island to take charge. ...(Sam) Subin, recounting the history of the organization, noted that he was a major promoter of the medical center because, before coming to Door County, he had served two years on a hospital ship. The contrast between this experience and the lack of medical facilities in the northern part of the county was, to him, especially striking."

Doc's long time friend, Pete Oleson said, "I think it was financial. He and Ruby had reached an age where he had probably not accumulated much for retirement, and had been offered better incentives there."

Doc was 53 at the time, and I'm sure his age played a big part in the decision to move; of course, he didn't leave his Island patients in the lurch. One day a week, Doc Farmer and Dr. Dorchester (from Sturgeon Bay) flew up to the Island in Dr. Dorchester's plane. Doc had patients come to the West Harbor Resort for appointments. (His office was in what is now Marianna and Herb Gibson's computer room. Herb still has Doc's desk/surgery table.) And

Doc Farmer Doc Farmer Doc Farmer Doc Farmer Doc Farmer Doc Farmer Doc Farmer Doc Farmer Doc Farmer Doc Farmer Doc Farmer Doc Farmer

146

when Islanders needed to see Doc, other days of the week, they took a ferry to the mainland and drove to Doc's office.

Herb with Doc's Surgery Table

Doc bought a beautiful old stone home on Highway 42. Luckily, it had four acres which supported Doc's gardening habit. Sister Bay and the rest of Door County appreciated Doc as much as the Islanders. He, true to form, gave 150% to the job as told by his friends and co-workers.

Doc Farmer Doc farmer Doc Farmer Doc farmer Doc Farmer Doc farmer Doc Farmer Doc farmer Doc Farmer Doc farmer Doc Farmer Doc farmer

147

"I know your character and methods too well, for I have followed your work for some years."
—Mrs. Ronder to Sherlock Holmes in 'The Adventure of the Veiled Lodger'

Prescription for Friendship

Pete Oleson was born on Washington Island in 1927, and stayed there through 1942. He met Doc Farmer on Doc's first tour of duty on the Island.

"Even back then, Doc treated my Mom for a badly burned arm, saving it from severe distortion," Pete explains. "I never saw Doc again until my brother Emery contacted me in Kaukauna that Doc, after moving to Sister Bay, was looking for someone to work with him, since the pharmacist there was retiring. Doc and I started on the same day, June 10, 1957.

We stayed working together until his retirement. I was at Bunda's Drug Store for 30 years.

Since Doc already knew me, it was a great relationship from day one in Sister Bay. On the Island, he not only had to charge for the office call but when needed, the drugs had to be furnished as well. Doc often threw in the medicine; it was very unprofitable over time. In

Doc Farmer Doc farmer Doc Farmer Doc farmer Doc Farmer Doc farmer Doc Farmer Doc farmer Doc Farmer Doc farmer Doc Farmer Doc farmer

148

Sister Bay, he could avoid the drug part, and concentrate on his practice only.

His practice was a huge success from the start. They had an office ready for him and the overhead was minimal. Patients loved him because of the attention he gave them, his informal personality, and usually the correct diagnosis. Back in the 1958 era, migrants still came to northern Door County in July and August for cherry picking. This was not what Doc needed. He not only had a big daytime practice, but had to take care of their maladies as well. This involved stitching migrants up at night from fights to delivering babies all hours. I remember how he and Ruby would be out there at night and after the delivery, Doc would go to the office with little sleep while Ruby would shop for needed items, including clothing, for the newborn.

In many cases this was done with no payment from the migrants. They had very little, if any, money before picking ended. This went on year after year. All this, plus the influx of summer tourists made for little rest for him in those months. Yet, we always tried to sneak in parties for diversion. I'm sure the summers, aside from migrants, provided income for him that had been denied for years.

And now for some things that made him a legend in Door County:

Doc Farmer Doc farmer Doc Farmer Doc farmer Doc Farmer Doc farmer Doc Farmer Doc farmer Doc Farmer Doc farmer Doc Farmer Doc farmer

149

His patients couldn't help but like him. No matter what, he made them feel at ease, and they left knowing that he was concerned for them. He had receptionists that were there to charge and run the office, but before the patient got to them for a usual charge, he would say in many cases, "Oh, Make it $__." That was a little hard on office procedure. Of course, most also had to hear Doc's latest "stories," some of which were, you might say, "off-color" but I don't think many were offended. Word was already out that his stories and jokes were expected as part of the visit.

Door County is long and narrow, and this was also a detriment for Doc. His practice stretched from Gills Rock up to Jacksonport and almost Egg Harbor. People coming during the day at the office were not a problem, but if he had to make a call, at night (which was all the time) it made for a lot of lost sleep that he really needed.

Treating patients at the county nursing home in Sister Bay additionally reduced Doc's rest time. This was during the infancy of nursing homes, when patients received care for about $150.00/mo and without all the rules and regulations. Anyway, Doc would unload his morning routine, and instead of relaxing for an hour, would call on twenty to thirty patients at noon hour and then go back to a full afternoon office routine. This, along with the other things

Doc Farmer Doc farmer Doc Farmer Doc farmer Doc Farmer Doc farmer Doc Farmer Doc farmer Doc Farmer Doc farmer Doc Farmer Doc farmer

150

I mention, will substantiate that his health was affected by his dedication.

In earlier days, a Doctor of Osteopathy did not enjoy the same respect that M.D.'s had, as they have today, so Doc did not have hospital privileges. He needed someone to consult or send patients to for a double check and for them to be hospitalized, if needed, someone he had complete trust in. He found this person in Dr. Jack March in Algoma, with hospital nearby. Jack was also a Cardiologist and it was a bonding friendship 'til Doc's death. Jack was a thorough physician, was pleasant with patients, and gave Doc complete follow-up. The horse was off his back."

"When Doc made house calls, he usually had his pipe along, but would often forget the pipe when leaving a call, so it would be hard to know just how many pipes he bought over the years."

"Then there were the cases of stitching a wound," Pete goes on to explain. "Doc's patients would tell me with a lot of humor they conjured up how Doc would say, 'You don't need an anesthetic for this little thing!' "Well, he didn't realize what 'chickens' he was working on."

Doc loved to be involved in politics or vent his opinion, sometimes, without weighing both sides. But most of the time, we understood. He also was an ad man's paradise! He was an avid reader, and if he ran across an ad, 'amazing new,' Doc had a check in the mail before he finished the ad. It was a good thing he had a large garage. Along with this penchant, Doc's generous attitude didn't contribute to his financial well-being either.

"I can't finish without mentioning his voice," Pete continues, "Doc was a good singer. We harmonized a lot whenever there was a party or get-together, and he didn't need coaxing.

Our office breaks at 10:00 a.m. and 2:30 p.m. at Al Johnson's were known throughout the Northern County. It attracted a lot of other business people and the conversations took in everything.

Doc was an avid gardener; one of the best! He used his hobby as his 'out,' but I was always on his back."

'Doc, it may be diversion—but you need rest,' Pete would tell him. "He never listened, and my opinion to this day is that he slowly died from 'burning out."

Doc Farmer Doc farmer Doc Farmer Doc farmer Doc Farmer Doc farmer Doc Farmer Doc farmer Doc Farmer Doc farmer Doc Farmer Doc farmer

152

Pete Oleson

Doc Farmer Doc farmer Doc Farmer Doc farmer Doc Farmer Doc farmer Doc Farmer Doc farmer Doc Farmer Doc farmer Doc Farmer Doc farmer

153

"Let us see whether by this purely mental analysis we can get to a finer point."

     –Sherlock Holmes 'The Adventure of the Three Gables'

Find It. Fix it. Leave it Alone

"Find it. Fix it. Leave it alone," was Doc's favorite prescription for health, according to Andrea Lundquist's memories. Andrea should know; she was Doc's medical assistant in Sister Bay for 8 years.

"I was hired by the Nor-Door Clinic fresh out of training at Northeast Wisconsin Technical College in June of 1969," Andrea smiles, remembering.

"Back in those days, we were trained to do a multitude of tasks covering all areas of need in a clinic setting. I handled the office procedures including helping patients with Medicare and insurance, assisting Doc with most of the patient's needs, giving shots, developing x-rays, performing lab work, doing many of the tests myself, assisting with tonsillectomies, and helping deliver babies, to name just a few. I remember how excited I was when Doc bought a new microscope and centrifuge for me.

Doc was a unique person. He was less refined than some in the medical profession, but

Doc Farmer Doc farmer Doc Farmer Doc farmer Doc Farmer Doc farmer Doc Farmer Doc farmer Doc Farmer Doc farmer Doc Farmer Doc farmer

154

he was also more caring to the community and its people than any doctor I knew."

Andrea goes on to explain:

"He had empathy, but now the medical world has become a business where money is to be made. Back then, if someone couldn't pay, Doc would say, 'Ok, just give me some of your vegetables or honey when it's ready.' Office visits only cost $4 then, and one could have an assisted birth for practically nothing. In the early 1970's Dr. Horrace Smith was hired to help with the work load and gave Doc Farmer a day off now and then. Dr. John Kordon, DDS, was the local dentist and also gave a compassionate and excellent service to the community. I remember when the clinic got a grant to hire a nurse practitioner/physician's assistant for a rural area, and Mike Flood came to be a primary part of the clinic. He later opened his own clinic, which is still in Sister Bay.

The doctors and the clinic—we were a very intricate part of the community. The ambulance was at Casperson's Funeral Home, next door to the clinic downtown, and the pharmacy was right up the road at Bundas.

Doc's daily coffee breaks at Al Johnson's Restaurant became infamous with Clyde Casperson, Pete Oleson, Sam Subin, Wally Mickelson, Al, and many others discussing the

Doc Farmer Doc farmer Doc Farmer Doc farmer Doc Farmer Doc farmer Doc Farmer Doc farmer Doc Farmer Doc farmer Doc Farmer Doc farmer

155

latest news, discoveries, politics, religion etc. This gathering was like clockwork!"

"Those years were some of the best years of my life," Andrea reminisces. "I was allowed to use my skills. I was trusted and I was taught. I was respected and had a voice. Doc wasn't critical or negative. He took the positive approach all the time. I felt so fortunate to be part of a community, and I knew everyone back then. Doc would also send me on house calls to draw blood for a test when the patient was too sick to get in. And I remember, tenderly, every Monday in the summer when Doc would bring in one of his beautiful roses from his garden and share it with his patients. They all commented on its beauty, and then on Friday, I would get to bring it home to appreciate for several more days."

"Oh, sure, Doc made mistakes, since he was human, but Doc cared tremendously," Andrea goes on to say. "Even to this day, because of the loyalty and dedication Doc gave to the community, he is loved. He is remembered mostly for all the good he did, and all those he helped. That will always override any unintentional mistakes."

"Doc was pretty consistent. He was good at diagnosing. If he didn't know he sent the patient on to the hospital. I had an ectopic pregnancy," relates Andrea, "and Doc treated me at home until it came to the point he had to

Doc Farmer Doc farmer Doc Farmer Doc farmer Doc Farmer Doc farmer Doc Farmer Doc farmer Doc Farmer Doc farmer Doc Farmer Doc farmer

156

refer me on. He and his wife, Margaret, were caring souls, and that came from inside. When I got home from the surgery, Margaret came to visit, delivering dinner as well. They were like that with everyone."

"Doc was dependable. He was always there for you. It didn't matter what time of day or night. He never took a vacation. An appointment wasn't needed at the clinic; if you called, we would fit you in. We worked on a first come, first served basis, and he stayed until everyone was seen."

"Doc handled everything—osteopathic adjustments, physical exams, pap smears, allergy shots, prostate problems, death, pregnancies and birth, tonsillectomies, lacerations, poison ivy, common cold and flu, and many farm accidents like chopped off arms in corn pickers."

"I helped him deliver thirteen babies. There was a hospital bed in the back room, and we kept everything clean and ready to go," Andrea continues. "Wow! I thought it was so amazing they had the baby and went home the next day; nowadays, its common practice to leave the hospital the next day. The big difference back then was that Doc would check in on the mother and baby at home."

When Andrea helped with the tonsillectomies, she would try not to gag along with the patients. Doc would use ether as his anesthesia, if he used anything. A lot of times, he would just use a tongue depressor, a local anesthesia and cut the tonsils out on the spot.

Doc's daughter Jane remembers when she was about nineteen that her dad took her tonsils out.

"He was an expert at removing tonsils. With a local and one snip Dad could peel those tonsils out like a grape. Three days later, we went out to a dinner meeting with Dad's colleagues in Green Bay. I was eating a regular meat and potato meal. Some of Dad's colleagues couldn't believe it. There were about twenty doctors looking down my throat at that dinner table. He received an A+ from his peers."

Andrea remembers Doc 'cracking' patient's backs.

"It would amaze me how Doc would come up behind you and tell you to relax," Andrea relates. "He would snap your back into alignment and you just felt 100% better."

Making people feel better was Doc's aim in life.

"This was his occupation and vocation," Andrea said. "He was comfortable. He wasn't out to be rich. The county was the perfect place for Doc."

Doc loved living in Door County Wisconsin and Door County loved him. He served the whole area from Sturgeon Bay, North, to Washington Island. Doc was called out

Doc Farmer Doc farmer Doc Farmer Doc farmer Doc Farmer Doc farmer Doc Farmer Doc farmer Doc Farmer Doc farmer Doc Farmer Doc farmer

158

all hours of the night and often the weather did not cooperate. On his hour and a half lunch, he would make house calls. When the summer people arrived, including the Hispanic migrant workers, his patient load doubled. Doc's daughter, Jane, remembers her dad coming home one evening with a sparkle in his eye and his heh, heh, heh laugh saying, 'I delivered a baby for Jesus and Mary today'. This was an Hispanic couple from Texas."

Andrea adds, "Anyone who was touched by Doc's presence, no matter what, gained something in their life that can never be forgotten."

Andrea Lundquist

"My old friend, here, will tell you that I have an impish habit of practical joking. Also that I can never resist a dramatic situation."
–Sherlock Holmes in 'The Adventure of the Mazarin Stone'

Smartest Man I Ever Knew

Dr. Jack March was a cardiologist in Algoma, Wisconsin. He was Doc's go-to-man when a patient had heart problems. Dr. March had hospital privileges so any of Doc's patients who had to be admitted would go through Dr. March. (Later, when Osteopaths were given full recognition as doctors, Doc was elected president of the staff of the Algoma Hospital. It was the first time in Wisconsin history that a D.O. was elected to that office on a medical hospital staff.) Every Wednesday on his day off, Dr. March would go 'up the county' with Doc making house calls. He and Doc had dinner together almost every Wednesday evening. He had great respect for Doc as he says:

"Smartest man I ever knew!" Dr. March says of Doc, "smart as hell! He had a knack for diagnosing problems by looking at you. He didn't always have the most up to date equipment or practices, but he could pull down an eyelid, check out the fingernails, or tell by the color of the blood what ailed someone."

Doc Farmer Doc farmer Doc Farmer Doc farmer Doc Farmer Doc farmer Doc Farmer Doc farmer Doc Farmer Doc farmer Doc Farmer Doc farmer

160

"Doc was a very devoted man," Dr. March adds. "On Wednesday evenings we would be sitting having a drink before dinner at Doc's home and invariably there would be a knock at the door. Someone needed Doc's attention."

"I remember one evening a fellow had a sickle cut. Doc told him to come on in and sewed him up with Coats #60 white thread right there at the kitchen table, all the while telling him, 'This won't hurt much.' Nothing daunted him."

"Doc was always sociable," Dr. March continues. "I never saw him mad. He loved music and loved to sing. His favorite song was 'Lay Your Head upon My Pillow'. Two drinks and he would start singing."

Jane said her dad loved to sing. 'Let Me Call You Sweetheart' and 'In The Evening by the Moonlight' were two of his favorites.

Mildred Goodman Jacobsen remembers going with her husband Paul to the Farmer's home and listening to classical music. Doc played saxophone in the Island Band and when he moved to Sister Bay he sang with a men's group. He would play big band tunes on the record player and just sit back, relax and listen.

Listening was one of Doc's fortes. He gave his full attention to his patients. Both ears were tuned in to you and only you, if you were his patient. He learned a lot by listening.

"Doc knew a lot of the life history of his patients," Dr. March confirms. "He prescribed natural remedies—herbs and vitamins. In fact, six of us were involved in a vitamin company called Midwest Natural Vitamin Company. Pete Oleson, being a pharmacist, pretty much engineered the company. This was in the days before vitamins became a popular item in drug stores."

"I formed the company," Pete Oleson said, "so Doc and Dr. March could work around the formulas they liked and we were paying too much for the ones available in most places."

Vitamins E and C were two of the vitamins Doc thought were so important especially for coronary care. He used bone meal to heal bones.

"It was a good excuse to get together socially," Dr. March adds. "The company lasted about ten years. It disbanded when Doc retired."

Doc was a meat and vegetables kind of guy. Dr. March remembers a trip they made around Lake Superior. There were all kinds of restaurants but what would Doc order?

"Doc would always have a steak," Dr. March recalls.

When Doc suffered a stroke, Dr. March took his office crew up to Sister Bay on Wednesdays to see Doc's patients. "I worried about his memory," says Dr. March.

"Doc's wife, Margaret, helped with the patients and she was always at Doc's side caring for him. They had a very loving relationship."

Doc Farmer Doc farmer Doc Farmer Doc farmer Doc Farmer Doc farmer Doc Farmer Doc farmer Doc Farmer Doc farmer Doc Farmer Doc farmer

162

"Doc and I had a very warm relationship," Dr. March explains, "I admired the man greatly."

Dr. Jack March

Doc Farmer Doc farmer Doc Farmer Doc farmer Doc Farmer Doc farmer Doc Farmer Doc farmer Doc Farmer Doc farmer Doc Farmer Doc farmer

163

"I can discover facts, Watson, but I can not change them."
    --Sherlock Holmes in 'The Problem of Thor Bridge.'

Waste Not, Want Not

Dick Burress is the Director of Emergency Services in Sister Bay. He remembers going to see Doc for sports' physicals, a broken leg from skiing and one night, a lesson in stitching.

"I remember one evening when I was 16; four of us kids were horsing around throwing snowballs. Craig Bastian ducked his head and hit his forehead, right near his eye, on the corner of the car door. We put a rag on his head and rushed him over to see Doc. It was about 8:30 p. m. and Doc's wife said he had just gone to lie down. Doc came out in his slippers and robe. He put Craig on the kitchen table, washed the cut with plain soap and water, and dried it. Before he started stitching, Doc said, 'Somebody had better stand behind him, he looks a little white!'"

When Dick became an EMT, Doc was still practicing in Sister Bay. One night Dick was sitting in Lyle Lundquist's squad car at the post office when a car went speeding through town. They took off after the speeding car. It turned out to be a Mexican couple and the guy was

Doc Farmer Doc farmer Doc Farmer Doc farmer Doc Farmer Doc farmer Doc Farmer Doc farmer Doc Farmer Doc farmer Doc Farmer Doc farmer

164

sputtering excitedly in Spanish. His wife was in the back seat, obviously in labor. Dick examined her and told them they would never make it to Sturgeon Bay. They probably needed to stop to see Doc. When they arrived at the Farmer's home, Doc said to Dick, 'you have to learn to do this sooner or later.' So Dick assisted Doc and this became Dick's first baby delivery.

Dick also remembers when the county ambulance service first started up that Doc was always supportive and a great contributor. One particular case, he remembers using the claw and hammer.

"There was a woman in the north end of the village that took in a woman boarder. This was before the Scand was in operation," Dick explains. "The boarder had gone into the bathroom and did not come out so the ambulance and Doc were called. When they got there, they could not get the bathroom door open because the woman had fallen against the door. They used the claw and hammer to make a flap big enough to crawl through, but the woman had already died. Doc could see the other woman was very upset and asked if she had any brandy. She came out with a bottle of brandy and Doc poured about an inch in each of four glasses. When Dick told Doc they were on duty and the two EMTs could not drink, Doc poured the brandy from the two glasses into his and the

Doc Farmer Doc farmer Doc Farmer Doc farmer Doc Farmer Doc farmer Doc Farmer Doc farmer Doc Farmer Doc farmer Doc Farmer Doc farmer

165

woman's glass and they both drank to 'calm down.'"

Dick goes on to tell about one peculiarity about Doc, something that couldn't be done in today's medical practice.

"When one of Doc's patients died, Doc would ask the family if he could take any of the unused medication and often ended up giving the medication to other patients who needed that particular med. It was tough on a medic who would make a subsequent call to a home where this happened. When the medic asked to see what medicines the patient was on, the bottle would have someone else's name on the script."

That would be Doc, always trying to save his patient's money and never ever wasting good medicine.

Doc Farmer Doc farmer Doc Farmer Doc farmer Doc Farmer Doc farmer Doc Farmer Doc farmer Doc Farmer Doc farmer Doc Farmer Doc farmer

166

"There is a thread here which we have not yet grasped and which might lead us through the tangle."

--Sherlock Holmes in 'His Last Bow'

Alive In Our Thoughts
(Special thanks to Lynn Mattke (Adeline's daughter) for permission to print Adeline's words. Lynn remembers Doc's heh, heh, heh laugh and stalwart compassion)

Adeline Edmunds wrote a book called, *The Living Spice of Life*. It was about her mother, Hedwig Augusta Heinrich Peil, and her journey from Germany to Door County, Wisconsin as a mail order bride. In the book, Adeline talks about a visit to Doc Farmer:

"Now going on eighty-eight the problems of age were apparent (for Hedwig)--eyesight dimming, steps getting slower, and memory lapses also. Tootsie decided that Grandma must have a physical and would take her to Dr. Farmer in Sister Bay. ...Dr. Farmer, a genial country-doctor, greeted her cordially and in his fun-loving way, said, 'Mrs Peil, am I to deliver a baby for you?'

With a quizzical look on her face, she replied, 'Ach no, Herr Doctor, I be too old. You should know better den dat, to ask such a foolish question--I jes no

*kin see too gut no more, und dats all dat be wrung mit
me.'*

*"Well, I'll take a look," was his reply. After
telling her glaucoma was setting in, she asked, 'Do dat
mean I will go blind?' He then assured her, "It may not
get any worse," and prescribed medication. It made her
happy when he finally said, 'Mrs. Peil, your body is
like an eighteen-year-old lassie and I'm sure you'll be
good for another ten years or more.'"*

What a marvelous word picture of Doc
and his outlook on life--genial, cordial, fun-
loving, assuring, prescribing and encouraging.
Doc could relate to Hedwig because their
philosophy of life ran along the same paths.
Adeline explains Hedwig's philosophy this way:

*"It is in life what you give of yourself to
others; in serving with love and understanding (not a
bounden duty) that brings joy to your heart. You first
must feel the pain in your own heart to know the
needs of others. In serving thus, you are accomplishing
what God would have you do. We carry our burdens
and help others to carry theirs. Life at best is a
struggle from birth to death. It is what we make of
our lives, and how we use our God-given talents, that
others may benefit in having known you. Thus we live
in their thoughts, also, and when a good person dies*

Doc Farmer Doc farmer Doc Farmer Doc farmer Doc Farmer Doc farmer Doc Farmer Doc farmer Doc Farmer Doc farmer Doc Farmer Doc farmer

168

believing in God's word, in faith and trust, he receives a crown at journey's end."

We 'others' have definitely benefited from knowing Doc. He used his 'God-given talents' serving us 'with love and understanding' that brought 'joy to us' and hopefully to his heart as well. His crown is bejeweled with many facets of sacrifice. Thanks Doc for helping us carry our burdens. You live in our thoughts.

Doc discusses medication for one of his patients

Milwaukee Journal, dated 1 June 1975, R. Brodzeller photographer, © 2007 Journal Sentinel Inc., reproduced with permission

Doc Farmer Doc farmer Doc Farmer Doc farmer Doc Farmer Doc farmer Doc Farmer Doc farmer Doc Farmer Doc farmer Doc Farmer Doc farmer

169

"My dear Watson, you as a medical man are continually gaining light as to the tendencies of a child by the study of the parents. Don't you see that the converse is equally valid? I have frequently gained my first real insight into the character of parents by studying their children"

-Sherlock Holmes in 'The Adventure of the Copper Beeches'

Family

Family was very important to Doc. During his life, he had three wives and three children. With his first wife, he had his only son, Edward C. Farmer, Jr. After Dorothy and Doc divorced, the relationship between Doc and his son became estranged. Doc was very proud of Eddie's piano playing and the fact that he was the youngest to graduate from the US Coast Guard Academy.

Ruby Larson and Doc married in 1940. They lost their first daughter, Jewel Ida to a congenital heart deformity. Doc treasured his next two daughters, Sara Doris, born September 1942 and Jane Ann, born January 1948. Although Doc gave most of his time to his patients, Jane remembers her dad always trying to be there for family lunches, suppers and band concerts. He loved his girls very much and was very proud of them.

Doc Farmer Doc farmer Doc Farmer Doc farmer Doc Farmer Doc farmer Doc Farmer Doc farmer Doc Farmer Doc farmer Doc Farmer Doc farmer

170

It must have been quite a balancing act for Doc and Ruby because Ruby was Doc's helpmate nurse as well as home mate. She devoted her life to taking care of Doc, his children and us, the patients. When she developed migraines, she started trying to find medicine to relieve the headaches. She had a brain tumor and died in August 1967. In the earlier years, her devotion to nursing was just as true as Doc's devotion to Osteopathy. Many of the Islanders remember her as warmly as Doc.

As an example of her caring ways, when Gert Young was going to have a fifth baby, she had not bought any baby girl clothes because, after all, she had four boys. She figured this fifth baby would be a boy also. When Vicki was born, Ruby couldn't stand for the baby girl not to have a little girl outfit, so she went out and bought one.

After Ruby died, Doc married Margaret Hanson Weborg in November of 1967. The love of Washington Island may have been one attraction between Doc and Margaret, because Margaret was born on the Island. Another attraction was that they knew a lot of the same people in the county. But the main attraction for Doc was Margaret's kind heart.

Keta Steebs spoke of Margaret this way in her *Door County Advocate* article about 'Doc Farmer Day':

Doc Farmer Doc farmer Doc Farmer Doc farmer Doc Farmer Doc farmer Doc Farmer Doc farmer Doc Farmer Doc farmer Doc Farmer Doc farmer

171

"Margaret Farmer's voice, when she answers the phone on a blizzardly, below zero night, is, next to Doc's, the most comforting sound in the world. She listens sympathetically as one recites a litany of ills, assures the sufferer (or parents of the sufferer) her husband will be right over and, no matter what the time, Doc keeps Margaret's word."

Margaret was so good to Doc. They had a very loving relationship and Margaret became Doc's caregiver after he suffered his first stroke in 1978. In 1979, Doc received a 50 year award for medical practice. In 1979, Doc suffered another stroke on New Year's Eve and died January 3, 1980.

Bless Doc's family and many thanks to them for letting us be a part of his extended family.

Margaret and Doc Farmer

Doc Farmer Doc farmer Doc Farmer Doc farmer Doc Farmer Doc farmer Doc Farmer Doc farmer Doc Farmer Doc farmer Doc Farmer Doc farmer

172

"Stand with me upon the terrace, for it may be the last quiet talk that we shall ever have."

--Sherlock Holmes in 'The Last Bow'

The Last Bow

So, we have come full circle making house calls with Doc. Walking in the Door, we stirred up some memories. We learned that everyone knew the same Doc--informal, tough, caring, devoted, compassionate, kind, generous, sociable, nurturing, loving, loyal, dedicated, prompt, unassuming, underpaid, singer, poet, musician, reader, woodworker, gardener, hunter, father, good diagnostician and consummate healer.

In his worn black satchel, along with his pipe and prescription for healing, came common sense, laughter, concern, trust, a listening ear, courage, devotion, empathy, knowledge, a bottle for calming the nerves, and a loving nurturing heart.

He definitely was not a saint (and I think most of the foregoing pages prove that), but he was loyal to his calling, his patients and his own ideals of what a human being should be. He did not let money be his ruler. He did not compromise the Law for bureaucratic law. He

Doc Farmer Doc farmer Doc Farmer Doc farmer Doc Farmer Doc farmer Doc Farmer Doc farmer Doc Farmer Doc farmer Doc Farmer Doc farmer

173

treated all with genuine care, no matter how high or low on the economic scale they fell. He was empathetic and sympathetic to the varied ills of his patients.

No wonder he was a legend in Door County. No wonder we, his patients, choose to keep his memory alive. For when Doc walked in the Door, healing came in and burdens were carried out.

Doc died January 3, 1980, ten days after he turned seventy-five, of a massive stroke--a short life for a man long on giving.

As his daughter, Jane said, "Saying good-bye to my father was the hardest thing I've ever done so far in my life."

In conclusion, let's not say good-bye; let's 'file it away in our archives', like Watson did for Sherlock Holmes. And every once in a while, with a warm tender feeling in our hearts, let's revisit Doc and stir up some dust of memories.

Thanks Doc, it was a pleasure knowing you.

Doc Farmer Doc farmer Doc Farmer Doc farmer Doc Farmer Doc farmer Doc Farmer Doc farmer Doc Farmer Doc farmer Doc Farmer Doc farmer

174

Chronology

Date	Event	Location
December 23, 1904	Edward C. Farmer born	Saulte Ste Marie, Ontario, Canada
June 30, 1923	High School Graduation	Sault Ste Marie Ontario Canada
September 26, 1923 to May 31, 1928	Attended Chicago College of Osteopathy	Chicago, Illinois
January 18, 1928	Married Dorothy	Chicago, Illinois
May 31, 1928	Received Doctor of Osteopathy Degree	Chicago, Illinois
August 10, 1929	Edward C. Farmer Jr. born	Chicago, Illinois
1929-1933	Licensed in Michigan and practiced in Escanaba	Escanaba, Michigan
1933-1936	Licensed in Wisconsin worked on Washington Is.	Washington Island Wisconsin

Doc Farmer Doc farmer Doc Farmer Doc farmer Doc Farmer Doc farmer Doc Farmer Doc farmer Doc Farmer Doc farmer Doc Farmer Doc farmer

176

Date	Event	Location
September 25, 1936	Moved to Sturgeon Bay	Sturgeon Bay, Wisconsin
May 12, 1939	Reciprocal Endorsement by Texas State Board of Medical Examiners	Plainview, Texas
May 31, 1939	New Mexico Registration and Examination Certificate	Grants, New Mexico
July 10, 1940	Married Ruby Larson	Holbrook, Arizona
January 7, 1941	Daughter Jewel Ida born Died 2 days later	Grants, New Mexico
June 1941	Moved back to Wisconsin	Washington Island, Wisconsin
September 7, 1942	Daughter Sara Doris born	Sturgeon Bay, Wisconsin
January 6, 1948	Daughter Jane Ann born	Washington Island, Wisconsin
July 10, 1951	Completed 6 week course CCO	Chicago, Illinois

Doc Farmer Doc farmer Doc Farmer Doc farmer Doc Farmer Doc farmer Doc Farmer Doc farmer Doc Farmer Doc farmer Doc Farmer Doc farmer

177

Date	Event	Location
April 12, 1954	Became naturalized citizen	Green Bay, Wisconsin
1955-1956	Chairman Town of Washington Island, Wisconsin	Washington Island, Wisconsin
March 3, 1955	20 yr Charter Member Lions Club	Washington Island, Wisconsin
June 1, 1957	Moved to Sister Bay, Wisconsin	Sister Bay, Wisconsin
June 10, 1957	Started working at Nor-Door Clinic	Sister Bay, Wisconsin
August 30, 1967	Wife, Ruby died	Sister Bay, Wisconsin
November 11, 1967	Married Margaret Weborg	Sister Bay, Wisconsin
September 26, 1971	Granddaughter Heather Jane Kane (Seubert) born	Muskegon, Michigan
August 1, 1974	Granddaughter Amber Joy Ballweg (Martinez) born	Michigan
June 22, 1975	Doc Farmer Day	Sister Bay, Wisconsin
April 27, 1976	Granddaughter Laura Jean Ballweg born	Michigan

Doc Farmer Doc farmer Doc Farmer Doc farmer Doc Farmer Doc farmer Doc Farmer Doc farmer Doc Farmer Doc farmer Doc Farmer Doc farmer

178

Date	Event	Location
March 1978	Suffers stroke	Sister Bay, Wisconsin
June 1979	50 Year Award for Medical Practice from WAOPS	Sister Bay, Wisconsin
January 3, 1980	Doc Farmer dies	Algoma, Wisconsin
June 21, 2004	Great granddaughter Samantha Jane Seubert born	Virginia
January 24, 2008	Great grandson Michael Seubert born	Virginia
2008	Legend lives on through the voices of family and friends in *"Doc"* *Memories of Edward C. Farmer*	Washington Island, Wisconsin

Doc Farmer Doc farmer Doc Farmer Doc farmer Doc Farmer Doc farmer Doc Farmer Doc farmer Doc Farmer Doc farmer Doc Farmer Doc farmer

179

Books Cited

The Complete Sherlock Holmes by Sir Arthur Conan Doyle

Andersen, Hannes, *Washington Island Through The Years,* Jackson Harbor Press, Washington Island, Wisconsin, 2007

Blei, Norbert, *Door Way,* The Ellis Press, Peoria, Illinois, 1981

Booth, Martin, *The Doctor and the Detective,* Thomas Dunne Books, St. Martin's Minotaur, New York, 2000

Brandt, Kari Fitzgerald, *Seasons of a Farm Family,* JdK Productions, Ellison Bay, Wisconsin, 1996

Edmunds, Adeline, *The Living Spice of Life,* Tech-Data Publishing, Milwaukee, Wisconsin, 1980

Remen, Dr. Rachel Naomi, *Kitchen Table Wisdom,* Riverhead Books, an imprint of Penguin Group, New York, 1996

Steebs, Keta, *Door County Advocate Articles,* 1974, 1975

Doc Farmer Doc farmer Doc Farmer Doc farmer Doc Farmer Doc farmer Doc Farmer Doc farmer Doc Farmer Doc farmer Doc Farmer Doc farmer

180

Documents

Doc Naturalization Certificate, dated 1954

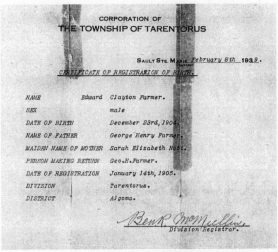

Doc's Birth Certificate

Doc Farmer Doc farmer Doc Farmer Doc farmer Doc Farmer Doc farmer Doc Farmer Doc farmer Doc Farmer Doc farmer Doc Farmer Doc farmer

181

About the Author

Martena Gunnlaugsson Koken was born and raised on Washington Island. She is an Islander even though she lives in the sleepy town of Ardmore, Tennessee.

Martena is an accomplished private pilot, and an avid horse woman with miles and miles of trail riding experience on her spotted saddle horse "Mac." Although she loves to engage in these sports, her real passion is writing. She writes poetry, and her short stories are aired regularly on the public radio station's "Sundial Writers Corner." One of those short stories "Sepia-Colored Dust," was the genesis for this book. Contact her at kokenfarm@ardmore.net

Doc Farmer Doc farmer Doc Farmer Doc farmer Doc Farmer Doc farmer Doc Farmer Doc farmer Doc Farmer Doc farmer Doc Farmer Doc farmer

182